Summer
INTO GROWTH

A Social-Emotional Learning Workbook for Tweens

Ages 9 - 12

Fun Activities to Understand Your Feelings, Make Good Choices, and Grow This Summer!

RICHARD BASS

HOW TO USE THIS WORKBOOK

Hey! This workbook is for you. There are no grades, no wrong answers, and no one is going to check your work. You can write whatever you honestly think and feel.

Here is what is inside:

- 35 fun activities across 5 chapters
- Drawing spaces, fill-in tables, checklists, and writing prompts
- Questions about YOU and your summer
- No boring stuff - everything in here is about real life

A Few Tips:

1. You can do one activity a day or skip around - it is up to you.
2. Be honest. This workbook works best when you say what you actually think.
3. If a question feels tricky, that is okay. Think about it and do your best.
4. You can ask a parent, sibling, or friend to do some activities with you.
5. There are no perfect answers. Just YOUR answers.

> **Summer is your time.**
> **Let's make it count!**

CONTENTS

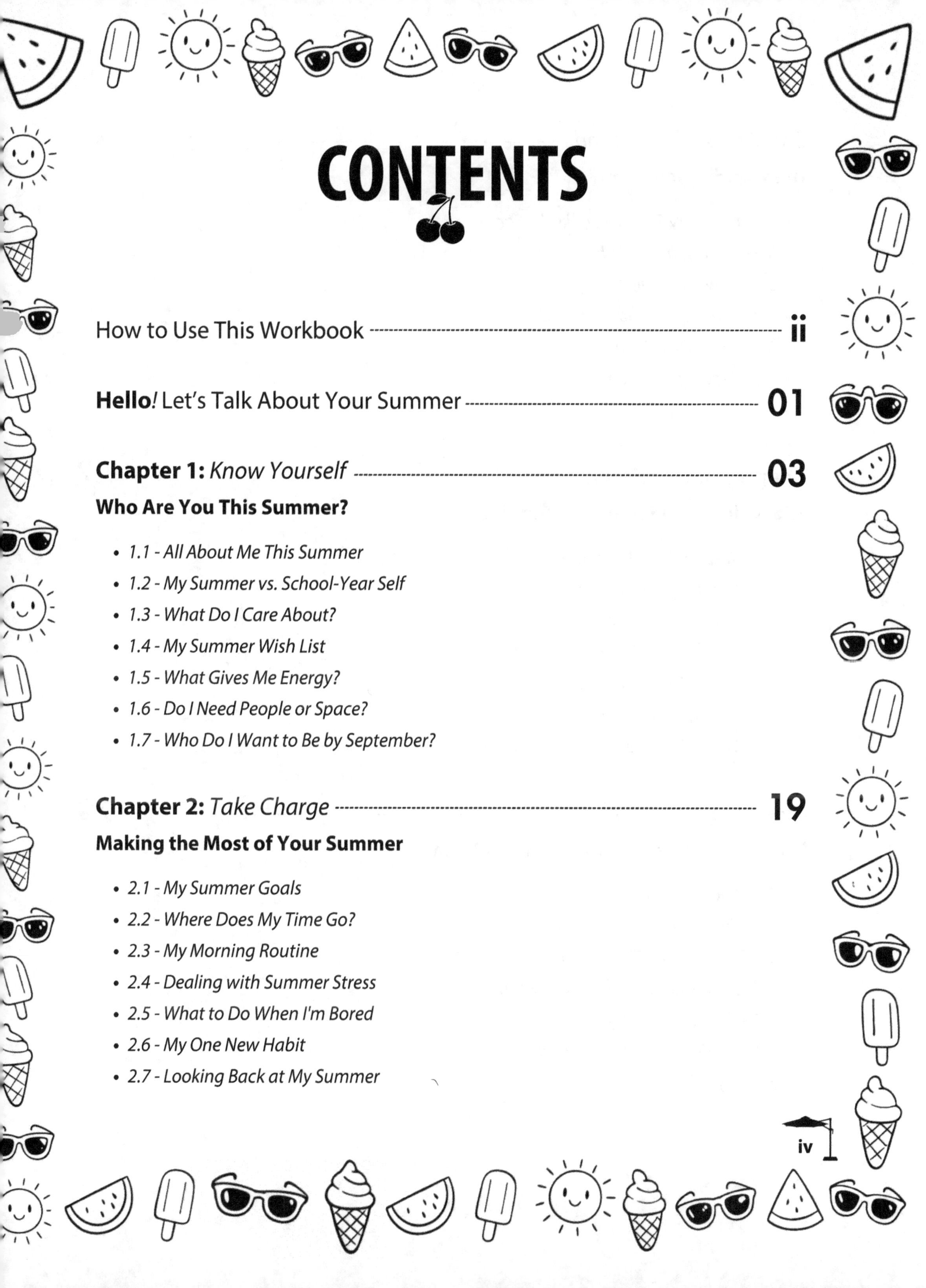

Who Are You This Summer?

- *1.1 - All About Me This Summer*
- *1.2 - My Summer vs. School-Year Self*
- *1.3 - What Do I Care About?*
- *1.4 - My Summer Wish List*
- *1.5 - What Gives Me Energy?*
- *1.6 - Do I Need People or Space?*
- *1.7 - Who Do I Want to Be by September?*

Making the Most of Your Summer

- *2.1 - My Summer Goals*
- *2.2 - Where Does My Time Go?*
- *2.3 - My Morning Routine*
- *2.4 - Dealing with Summer Stress*
- *2.5 - What to Do When I'm Bored*
- *2.6 - My One New Habit*
- *2.7 - Looking Back at My Summer*

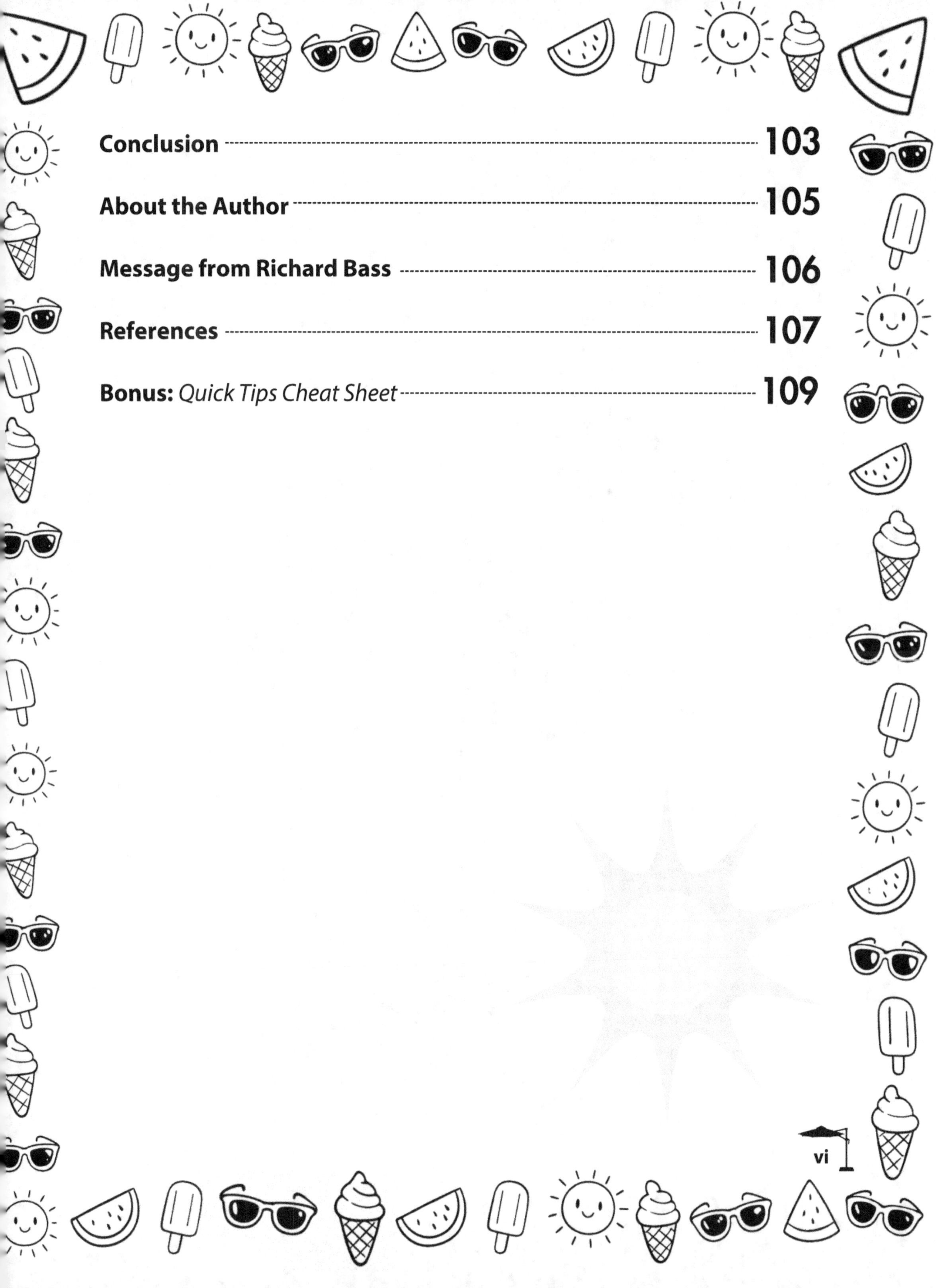

HELLO!

LET'S TALK ABOUT YOUR SUMMER

Summer is HERE.

No more alarm clocks.

No more homework.

No more rushing out the door every morning.

But here is something a lot of people do not talk about: sometimes summer feels amazing, and sometimes it feels... kind of blah. You might be super excited for three weeks and then run out of things to do. Or you might have so much going on that you feel stressed out instead of relaxed.

Either way - this workbook is here to help.

> *This is not a school workbook. There are no right answers. It is just a space for you to think, explore, and figure out more about yourself this summer.*

The five chapters in this book will help you:

- Understand yourself better (Chapter 1)
- Make the most of your free time (Chapter 2)
- Think about the people around you (Chapter 3)
- Build better friendships and family relationships (Chapter 4)
- Make smart choices this summer (Chapter 5)

Ready? Let's go!

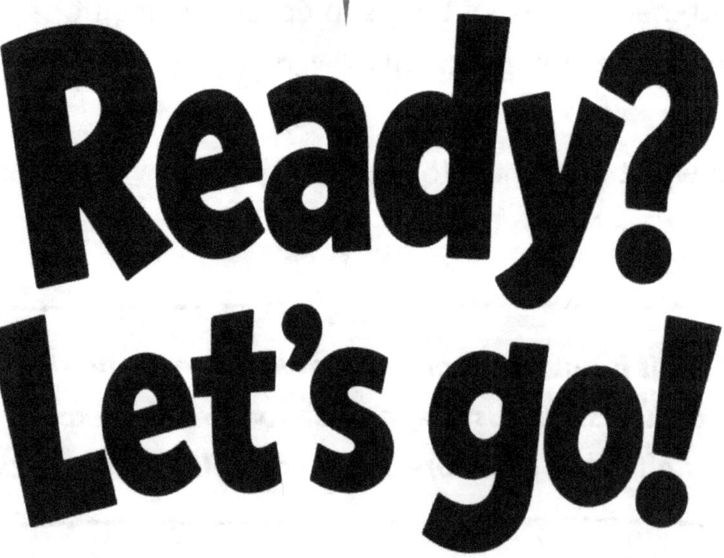

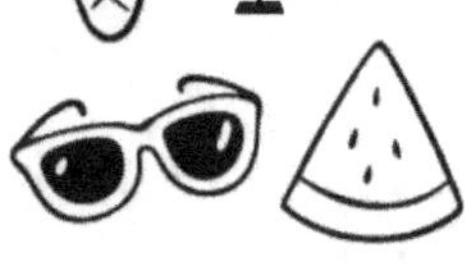

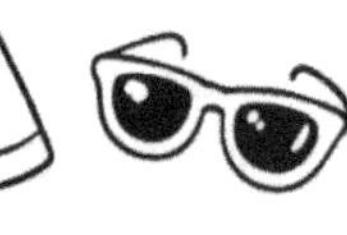

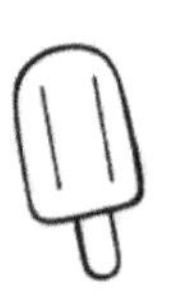

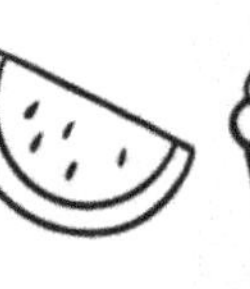

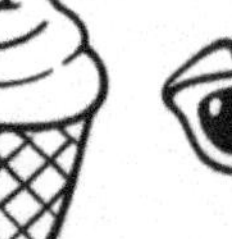

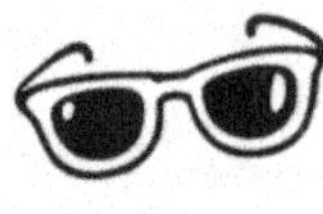

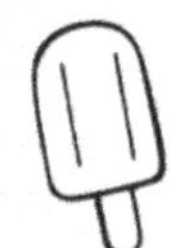

CHAPTER 1

KNOW YOURSELF

Who Are You This Summer?

Before you can have a great summer, it helps to know a little more about yourself. What do you like? What makes you happy? What kind of person are you when school is NOT telling you what to do?

These seven activities will help you figure that out. Get ready to think about YOU.

EXERCISE 1.1

ALL ABOUT ME THIS SUMMER

Let's start simple. This is your chance to introduce yourself - to yourself. Fill in the boxes below as honestly as you can.

My name is...	My age is...	My grade going into...

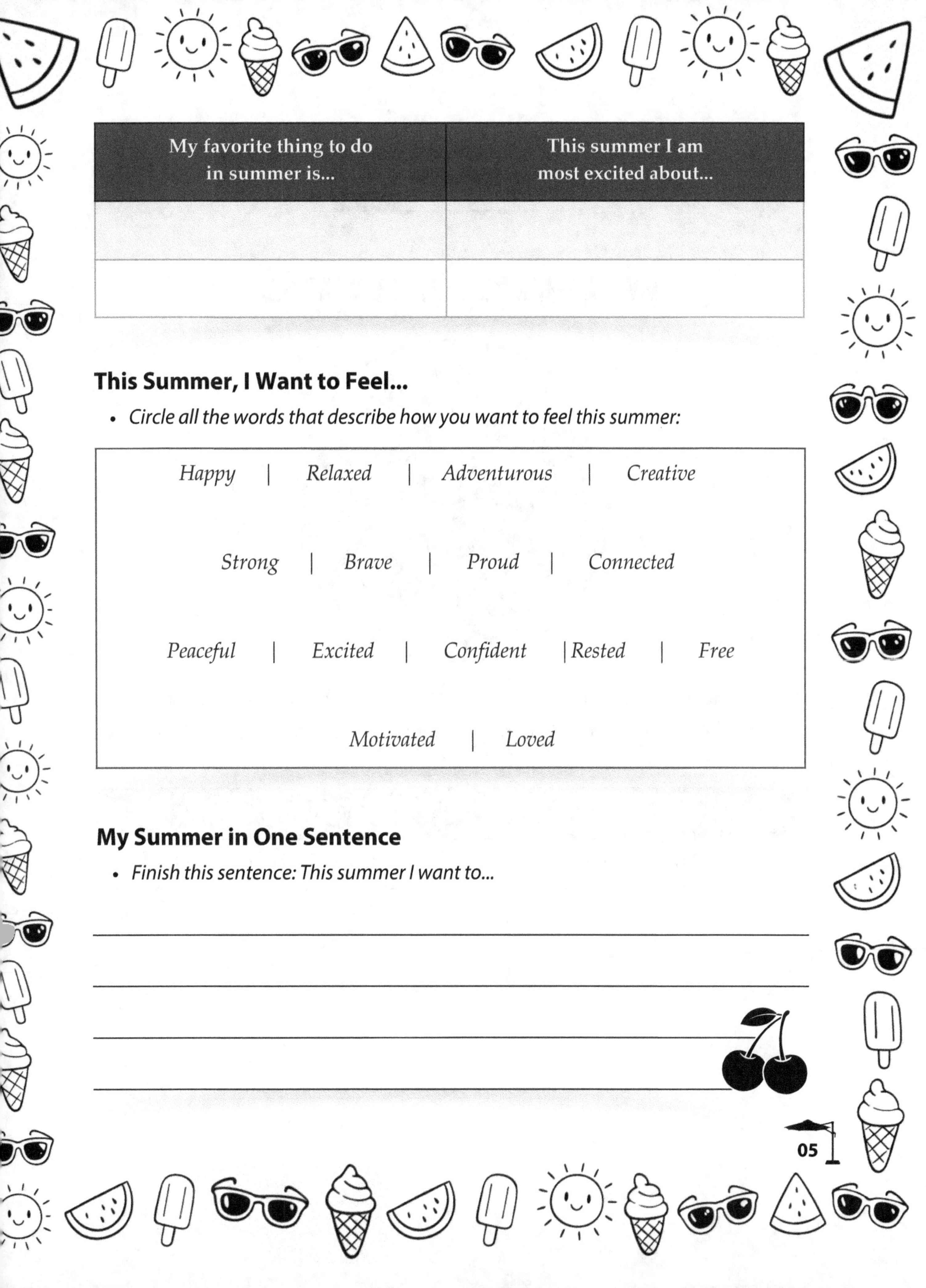

My favorite thing to do in summer is...	This summer I am most excited about...

This Summer, I Want to Feel...

- *Circle all the words that describe how you want to feel this summer:*

Happy | *Relaxed* | *Adventurous* | *Creative*

Strong | *Brave* | *Proud* | *Connected*

Peaceful | *Excited* | *Confident* | *Rested* | *Free*

Motivated | *Loved*

My Summer in One Sentence

- *Finish this sentence: This summer I want to...*

____

____

____

____

EXERCISE 1.2

MY SUMMER VS. SCHOOL-YEAR SELF

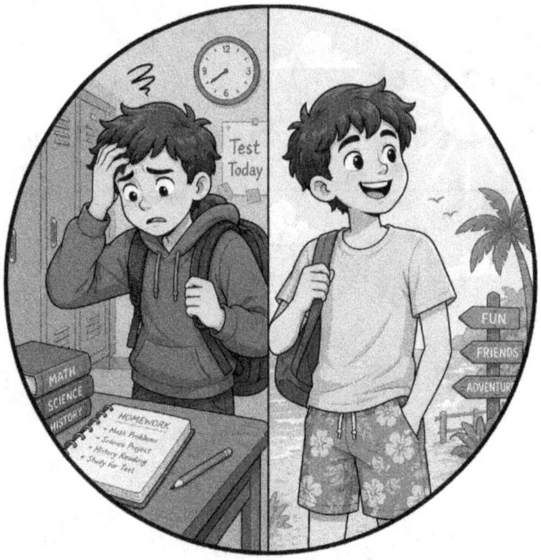

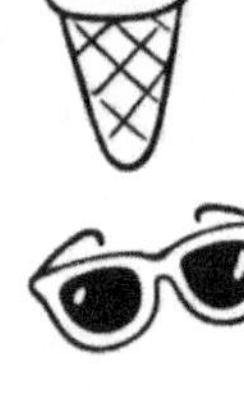

Did you know you can actually be a little different in summer than you are during the school year? That is totally normal! Summer lets a different side of you come out.

During the school year I am...	In summer I am (or want to be)...
Always in a rush	More chilled out (example)

My Summer Superpower

- *Everyone has something they are good at. What is YOUR summer superpower - something you do really well when you have free time?*

____

____

____

____

One Thing I Want to Try This Summer

- *It can be something small or something big. What is one thing you have never done before that you want to try this summer?*

____

____

____

EXERCISE 1.3

WHAT DO I CARE ABOUT?

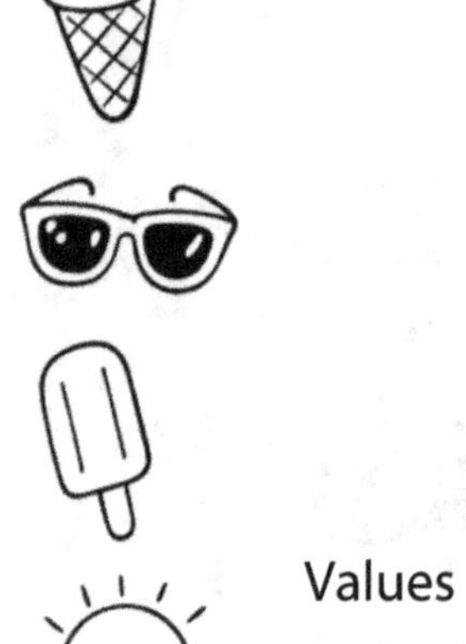

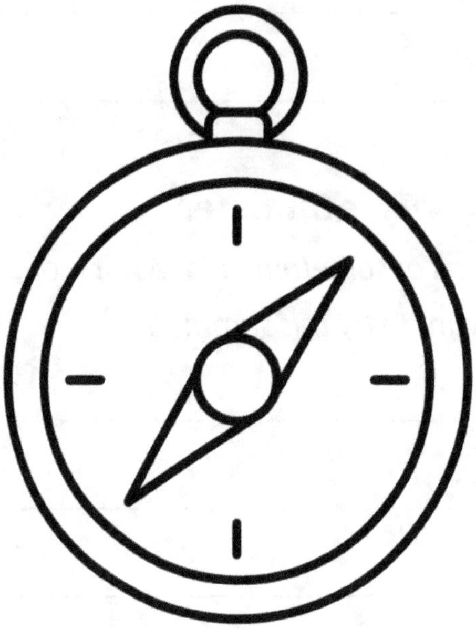

Values are the things that matter most to you. They are like a map that helps you make decisions. When you know what you care about, it is easier to choose how to spend your time.

Circle Your Top 5 Values

Family | *Kindness* | *Fun* | *Honesty* | *Creativity*

Loyalty | *Fairness* | *Hard Work* | *Adventure* | *Health*

Learning | *Humor* | *Freedom* | *Friendship* | *Respect*

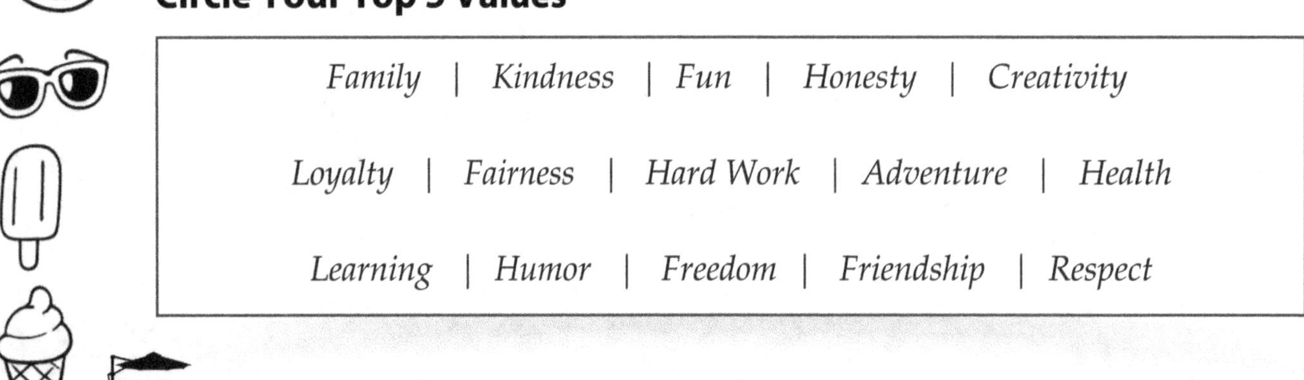

Write your top 5 here and say why each one matters to you:

1. _________________________________ • *Why* _____________________________

   ____

2. _________________________________ • *Why* _____________________________

   ____

3. _________________________________ • *Why* _____________________________

   ____

4. _________________________________ • *Why* _____________________________

   ____

5. _________________________________ • *Why* _____________________________

   ____

Values in Real Life

- *Think of something you will probably do this summer - like hanging out with friends, going somewhere, or working on a project. How does one of your values connect to it?*

____

____

____

MY SUMMER WISH LIST

A wish list is different from a to-do list. A to-do list is about chores and tasks. A wish list is about what you actually WANT to do, see, feel, and experience. Let's make yours.

Things I Want to DO This Summer	Things I Want to FEEL or LEARN

My Number One Wish

- *Look at your list. What is the ONE thing you would be most disappointed if you did NOT get to do? Circle it above, then write why it matters so much:*

____

____

____

____

My First Step

- *What is one small thing you could do THIS WEEK to make that wish happen?*

____

____

____

WHAT GIVES ME ENERGY?

Some things give you energy - they make you feel pumped up, happy, or alive. Other things drain your energy - they leave you feeling tired, grumpy, or blah. Knowing which is which helps you plan a great summer.

ENERGY BOOSTERS (things that make me feel great!)	ENERGY DRAINERS (things that wear me out)

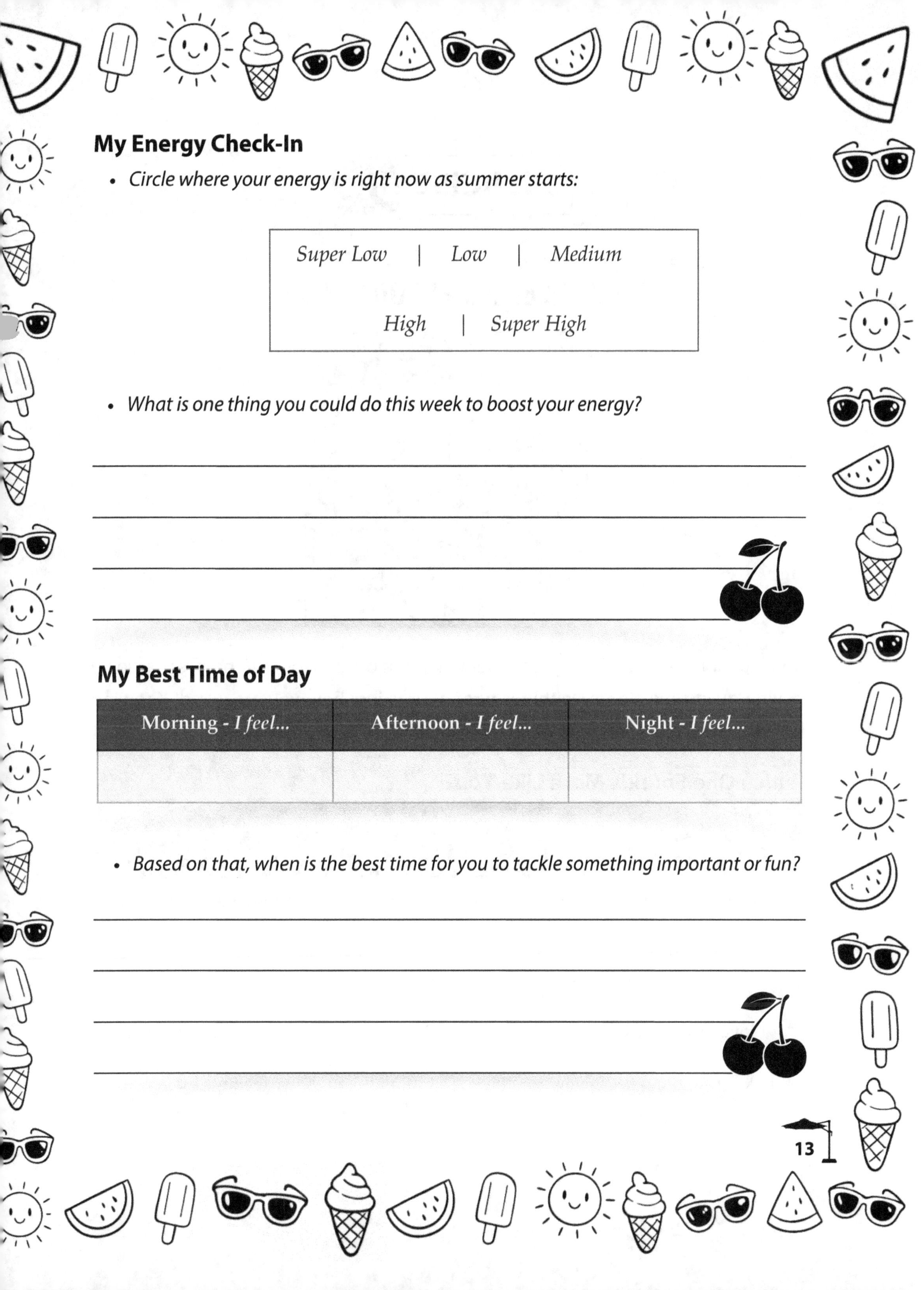

My Energy Check-In

- *Circle where your energy is right now as summer starts:*

Super Low	*Low*	*Medium*
	High	*Super High*

- *What is one thing you could do this week to boost your energy?*

____

____

____

____

My Best Time of Day

Morning - *I feel...*	Afternoon - *I feel...*	Night - *I feel...*

- *Based on that, when is the best time for you to tackle something important or fun?*

____

____

____

DO I NEED PEOPLE OR SPACE?

Some people get their energy from being around other people. Others recharge by having quiet time alone. Neither is wrong - it is just how you are wired! Knowing this helps you plan your summer so you actually feel good.

Which One Sounds More Like You?

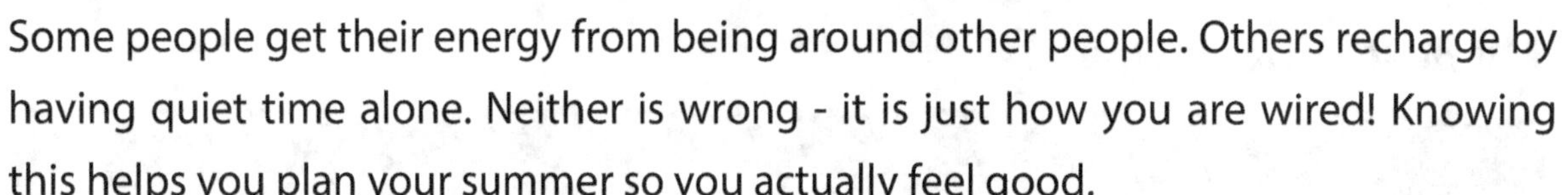

Team Player *(I love being with people!)*	Solo Explorer *(I love my own time!)*
I feel happy when I am with friends	I feel happy when I have alone time
I get bored when I am by myself too long	I get tired when I am with people too long
I love group activities and games	I love solo projects and exploring alone
I talk through my feelings with others	I think through my feelings by myself

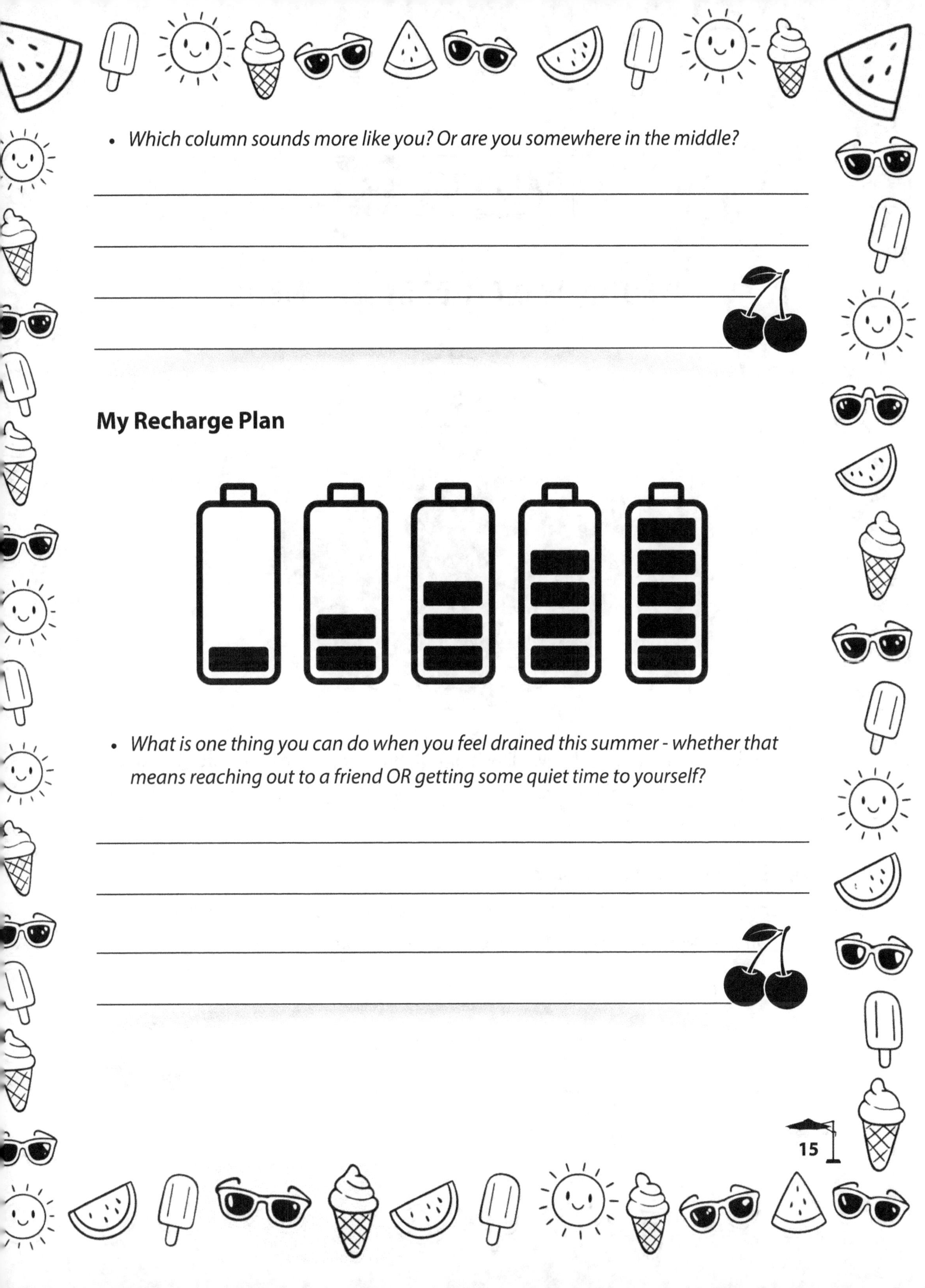

- *Which column sounds more like you? Or are you somewhere in the middle?*

____

____

____

____

My Recharge Plan

- *What is one thing you can do when you feel drained this summer - whether that means reaching out to a friend OR getting some quiet time to yourself?*

____

____

____

____

WHO DO I WANT TO BE BY SEPTEMBER?

September is coming whether we like it or not. But here is the cool part - you get to decide what kind of person you want to be when it gets here. Summer is your chance to grow.

My Summer Growth Vision

- *Imagine it is the first day back at school in September. You had an amazing summer. What is different about you? Fill in the blanks:*

I am better at:

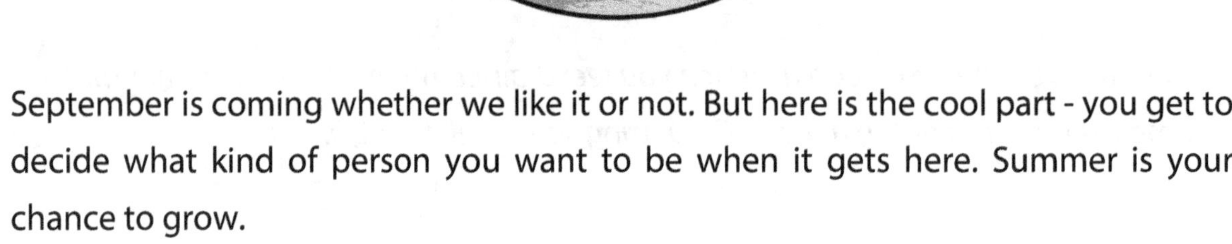

I feel more:

____

____

I tried something new - I:

____

____

I am proud that I:

____

____

My Summer Timeline

Early Summer (first 4 weeks)	Mid Summer (middle 4 weeks)	End of Summer (last 4 weeks)
I want to focus on:	I want to focus on:	I want to focus on:

CHAPTER 2

TAKE CHARGE

Making the Most of Your Summer

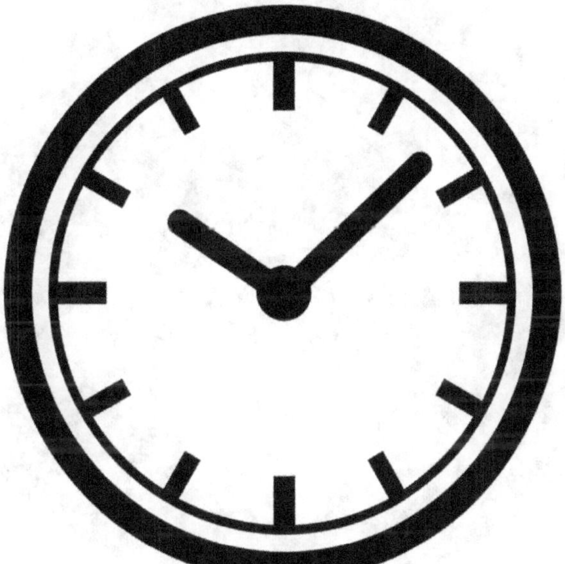

Freedom is awesome. But too much free time with no plan can lead to a lot of couch time and screen time - and before you know it, summer is almost over and you feel like you wasted it.

This chapter is all about helping you take charge of your summer. Not in a boring, grown-up way. In a YOU way.

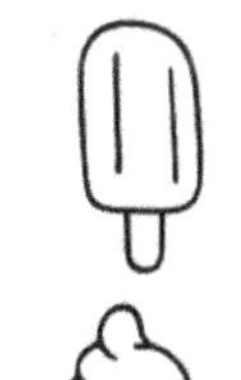

MY SUMMER GOALS

Goals are not just for school. Having a goal gives you something to look forward to and feel proud of when you reach it. Let's make your summer goals fun and real.

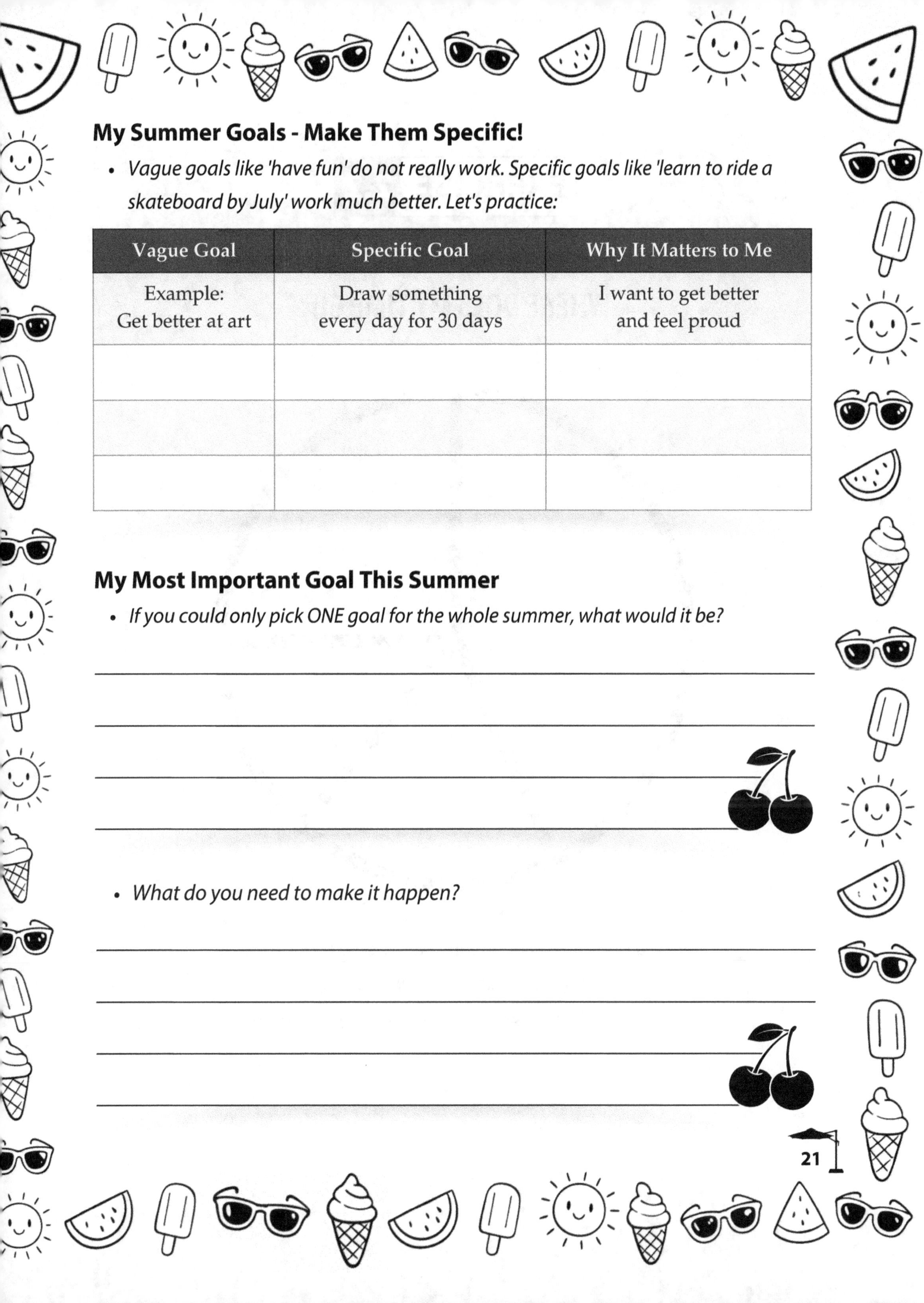

My Summer Goals - Make Them Specific!

- *Vague goals like 'have fun' do not really work. Specific goals like 'learn to ride a skateboard by July' work much better. Let's practice:*

Vague Goal	Specific Goal	Why It Matters to Me
Example: Get better at art	Draw something every day for 30 days	I want to get better and feel proud

My Most Important Goal This Summer

- *If you could only pick ONE goal for the whole summer, what would it be?*

____

____

____

____

- *What do you need to make it happen?*

____

____

____

EXERCISE 2.2

WHERE DOES MY TIME GO?

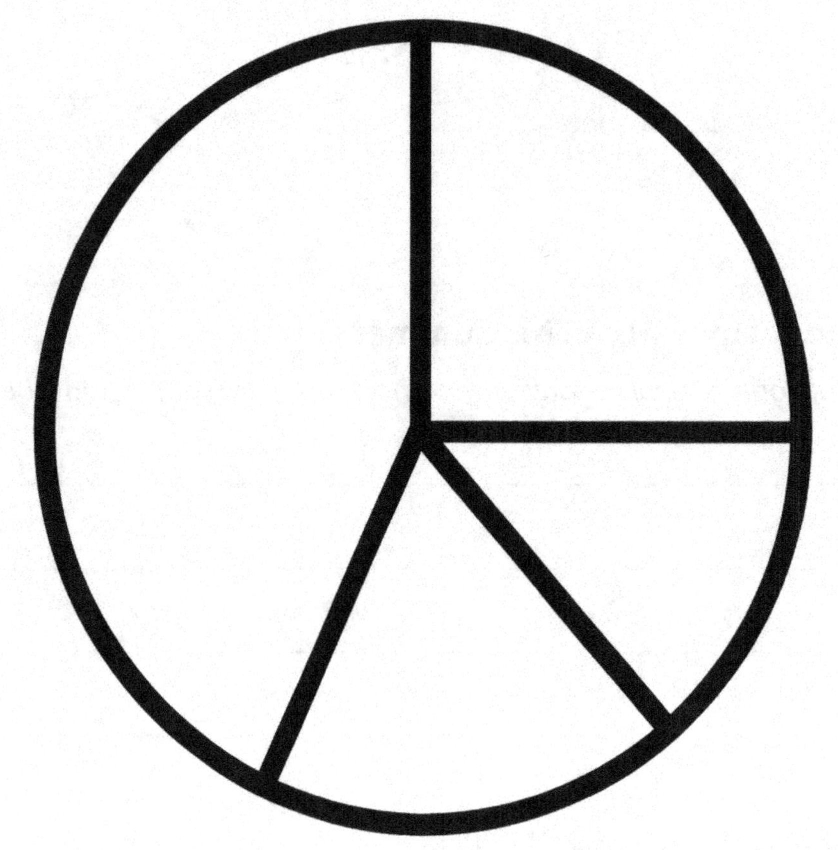

Here is a question most tweens have never thought about:
Where does your time actually GO each day?
Let's find out - and see if you want to change anything.

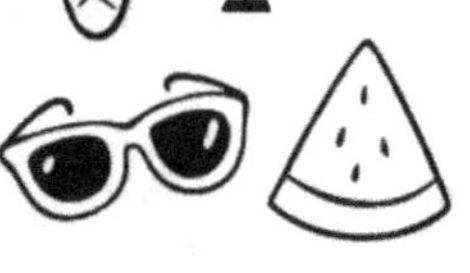

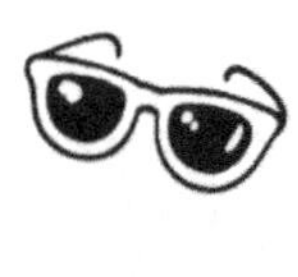

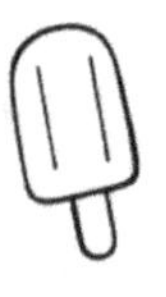

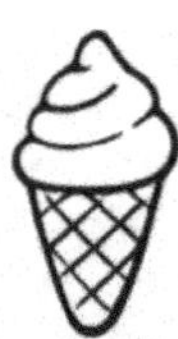

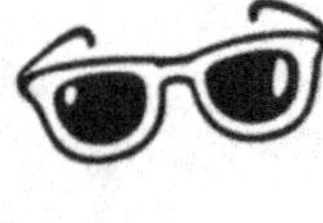

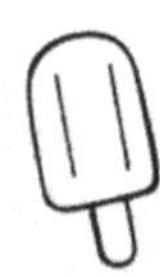

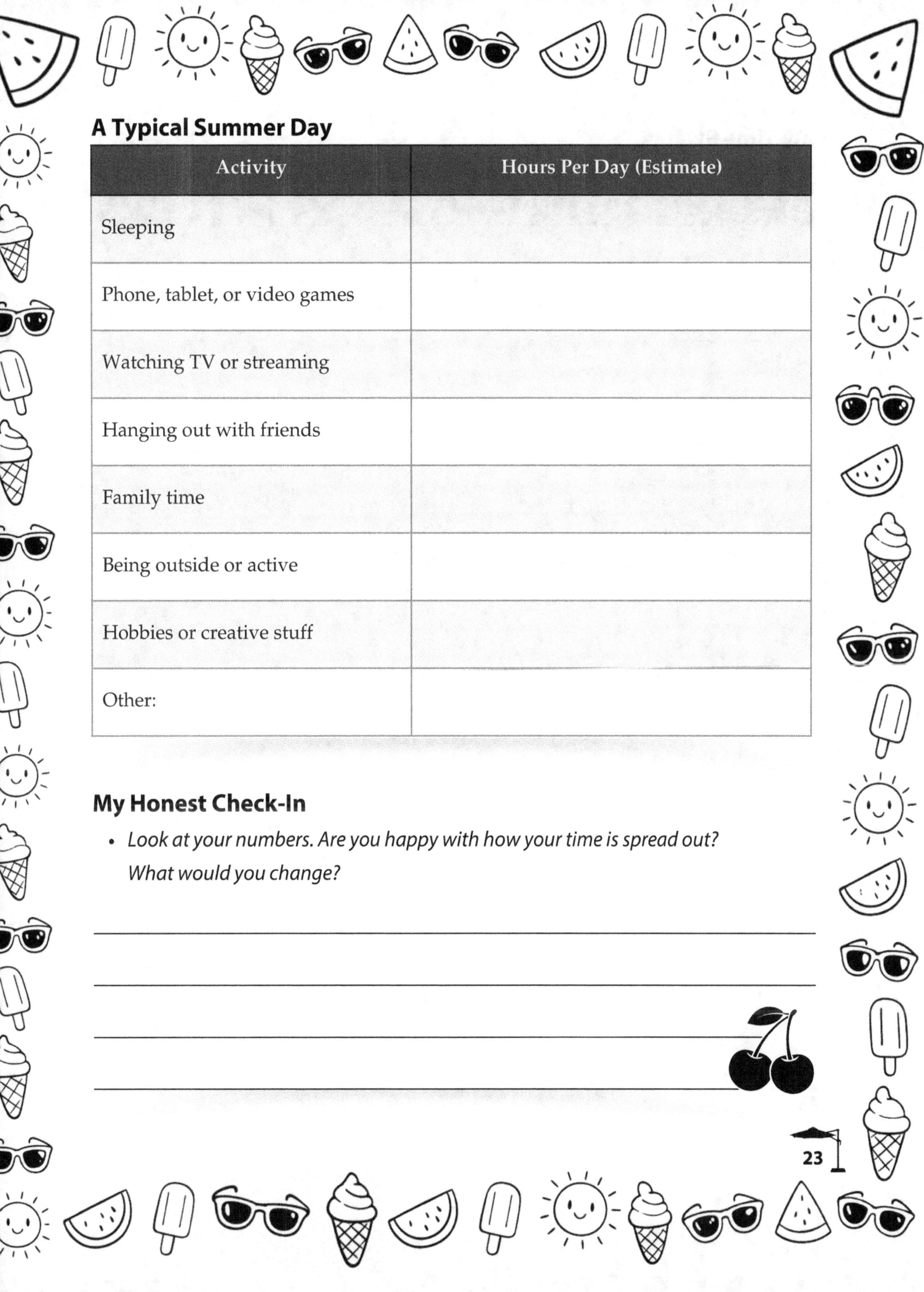

A Typical Summer Day

Activity	Hours Per Day (Estimate)
Sleeping	
Phone, tablet, or video games	
Watching TV or streaming	
Hanging out with friends	
Family time	
Being outside or active	
Hobbies or creative stuff	
Other:	

My Honest Check-In

- *Look at your numbers. Are you happy with how your time is spread out? What would you change?*

____

____

____

____

My Time Swap

I want LESS time on...	I want MORE time on...

MY MORNING ROUTINE

How you start your morning sets the tone for the whole day. A good morning routine does not have to be long or complicated - it just needs to help you feel ready.

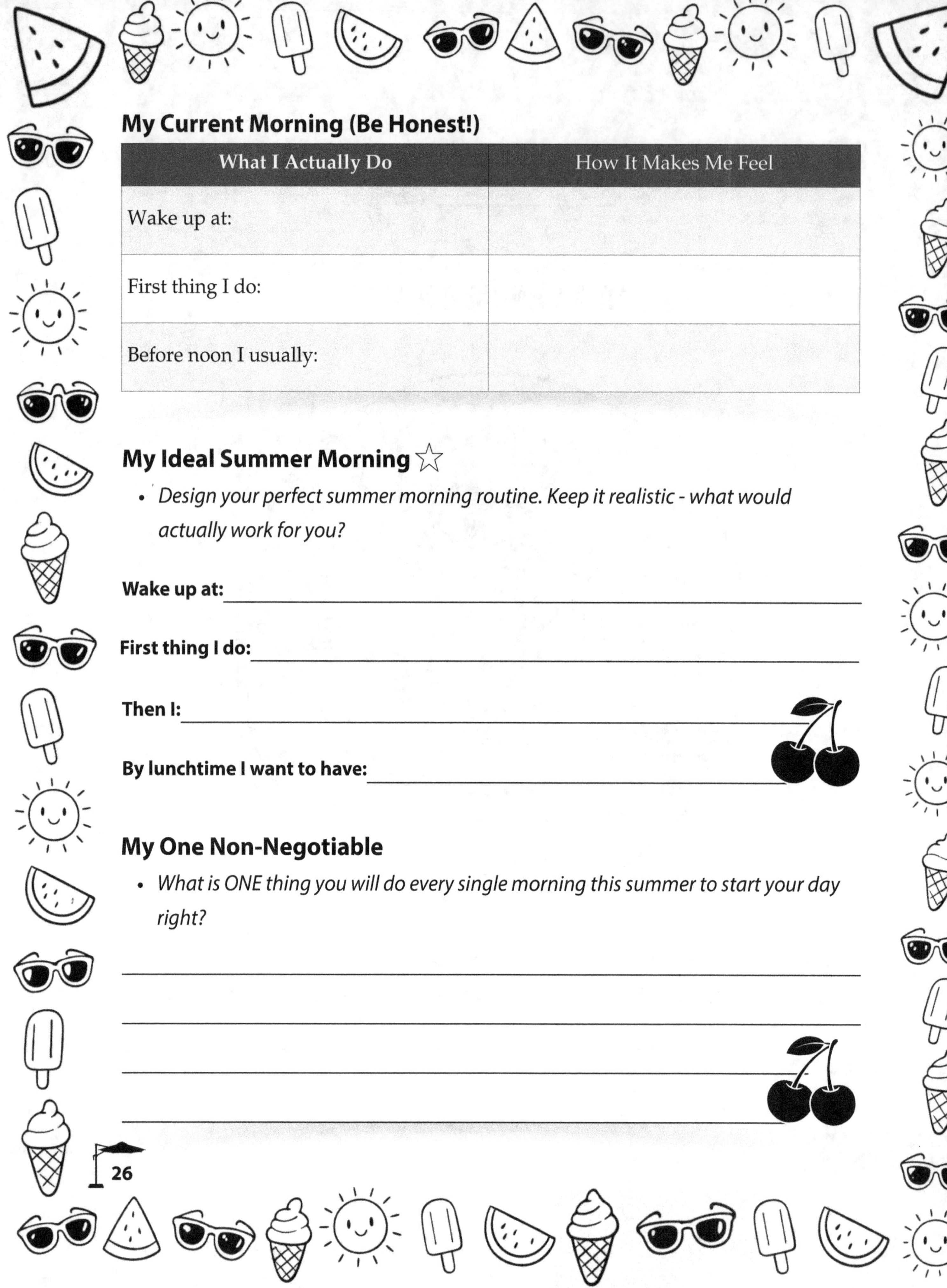

My Current Morning (Be Honest!)

What I Actually Do	How It Makes Me Feel
Wake up at:	
First thing I do:	
Before noon I usually:	

My Ideal Summer Morning ☆

- *Design your perfect summer morning routine. Keep it realistic - what would actually work for you?*

Wake up at: ____

First thing I do: ____

Then I: ____

By lunchtime I want to have: ____

My One Non-Negotiable

- *What is ONE thing you will do every single morning this summer to start your day right?*

____

____

____

DEALING WITH SUMMER STRESS

Even in summer, things can feel stressful. Maybe there is family drama, friend conflict, summer programs, or just the pressure of feeling like you should be doing something fun all the time. Stress is real - even in July.

What Stresses Me Out in Summer?

- *Check all that apply to you:*

    - *Family arguments or tension*
    - *Feeling left out of friend group plans*
    - *Being bored but not knowing what to do*
    - *Summer programs or activities I don't want to do*
    - *Pressure to be productive or not waste summer*
    - *Changes in routine or travel*
    - *Worrying about going back to school*
    - *Something else:* ____

What I Do When I'm Stressed

Things I Do That HELP	Things I Do That Don't Help

My Calming Strategy

- *Write one thing you can do the next time summer stress creeps in:*

____

____

____

____

WHAT TO DO WHEN I'M BORED

Being bored is actually really normal - and believe it or not, scientists say a little boredom is actually GOOD for your brain. It helps your imagination wake up! The trick is knowing what to do when boredom hits so you don't just scroll for two hours.

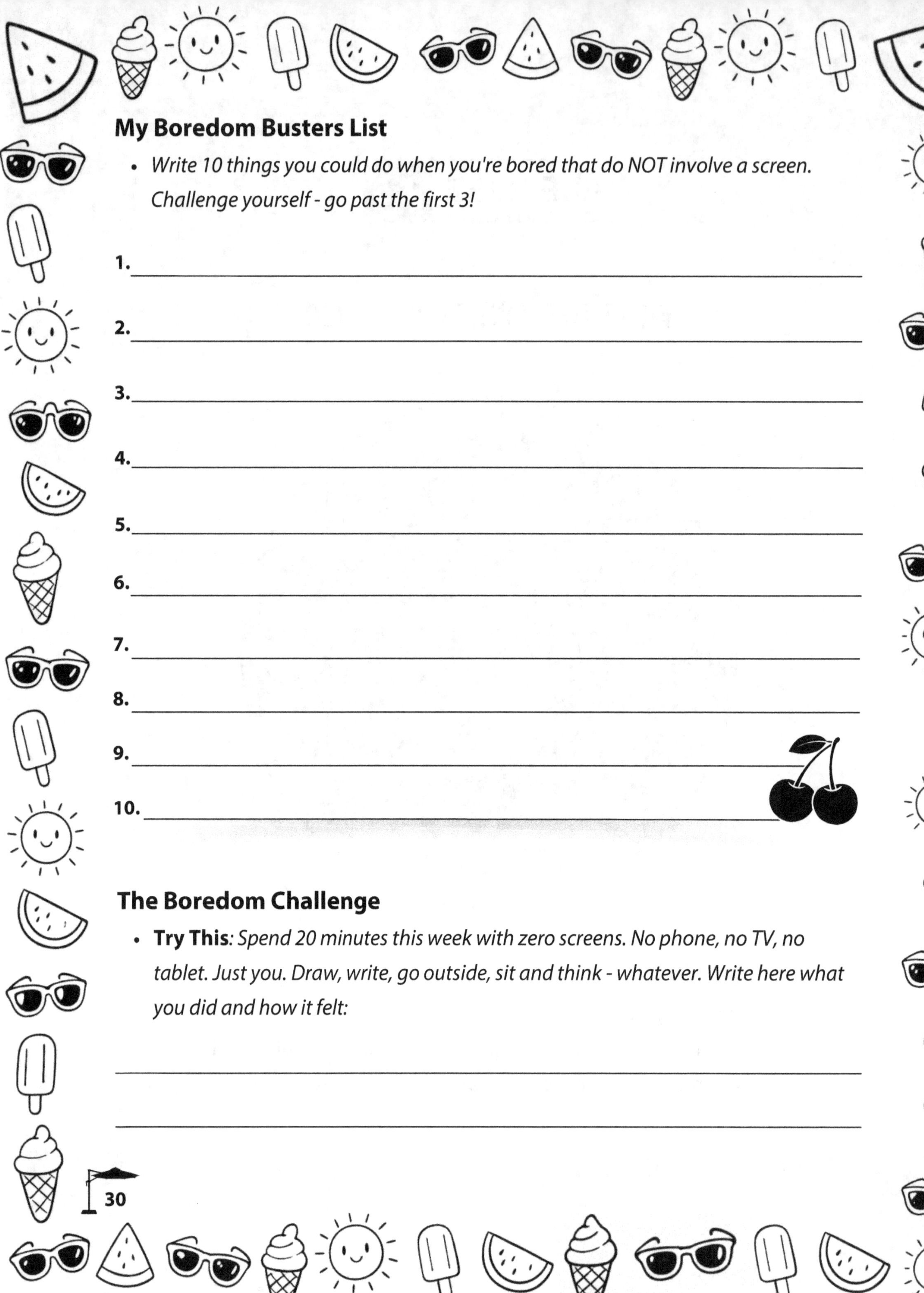

My Boredom Busters List

- *Write 10 things you could do when you're bored that do NOT involve a screen. Challenge yourself - go past the first 3!*

1. ____

2. ____

3. ____

4. ____

5. ____

6. ____

7. ____

8. ____

9. ____

10. ____

The Boredom Challenge

- **Try This**: *Spend 20 minutes this week with zero screens. No phone, no TV, no tablet. Just you. Draw, write, go outside, sit and think - whatever. Write here what you did and how it felt:*

____

____

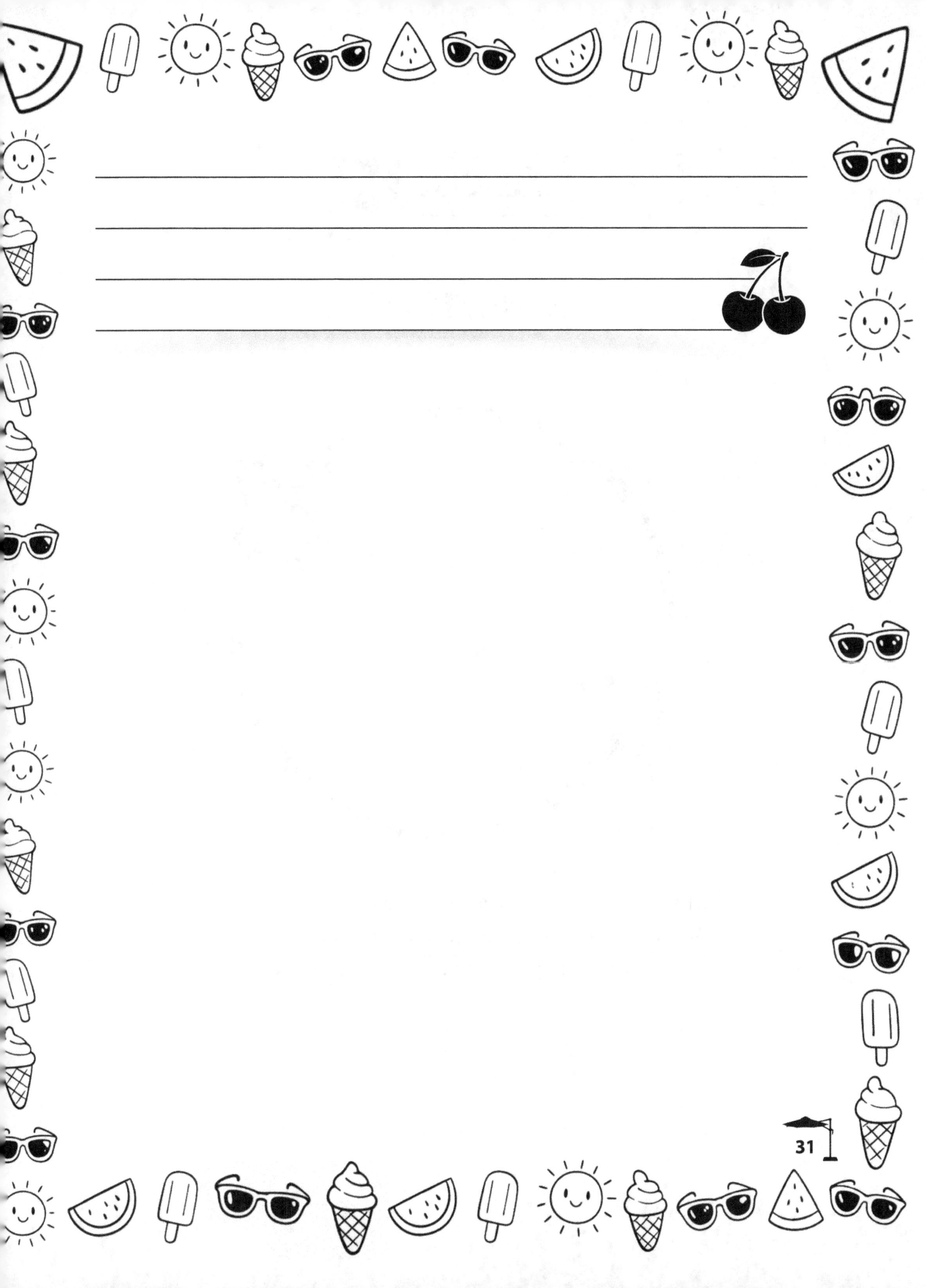

EXERCISE 2.6

MY ONE NEW HABIT

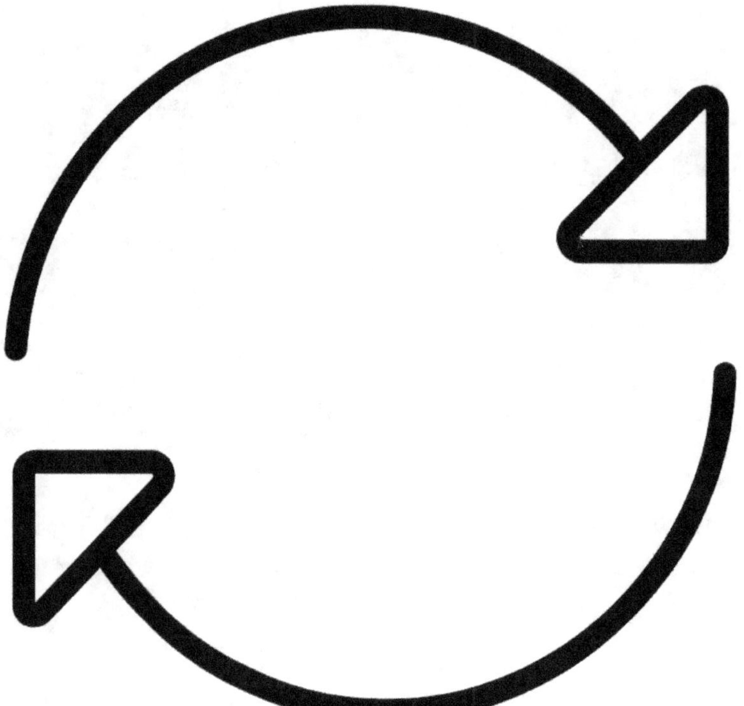

A habit is something you do so often it becomes automatic - like brushing your teeth. This summer you have time to build one new habit that could stick for life. What will yours be?

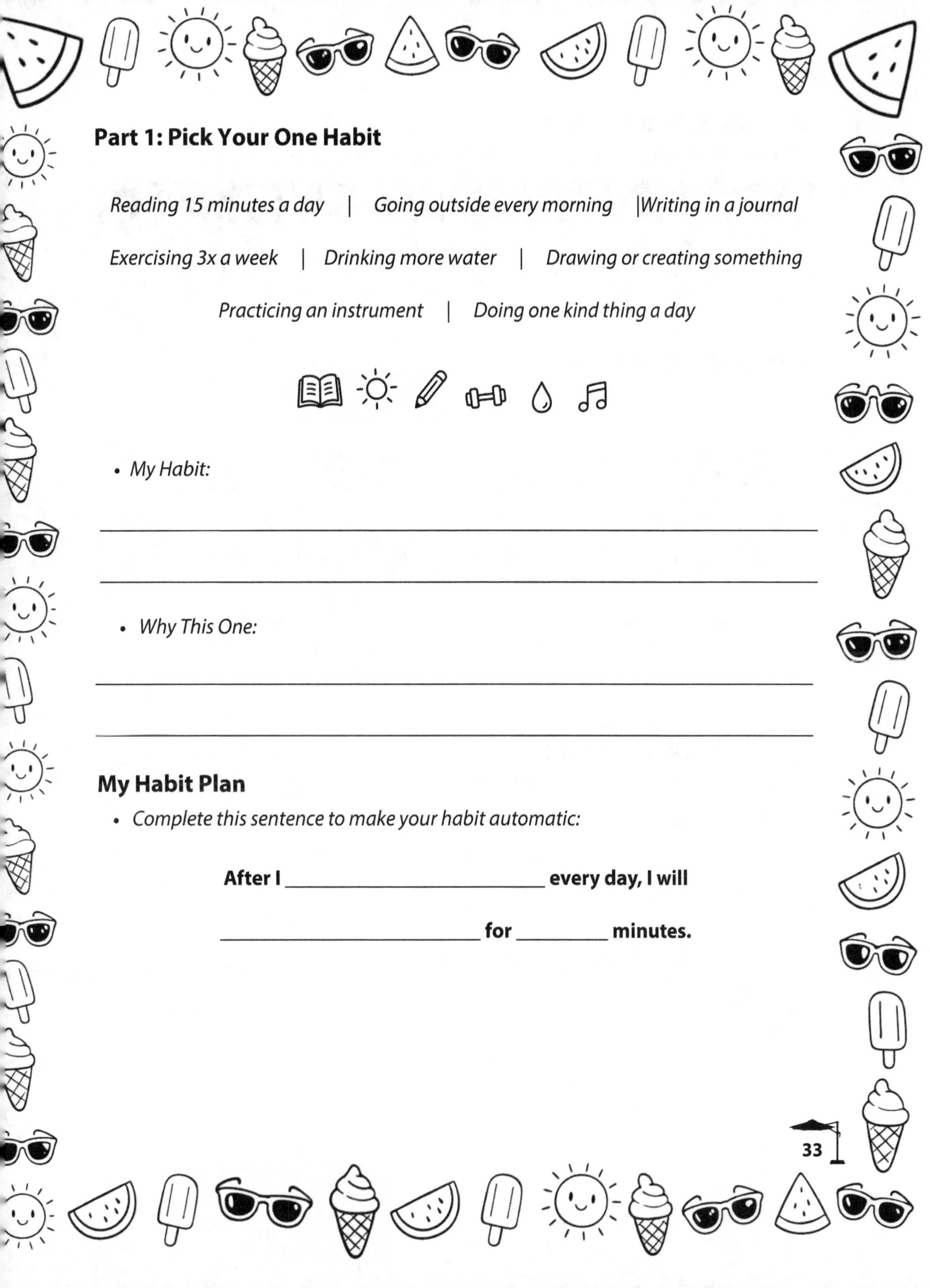

Part 1: Pick Your One Habit

Reading 15 minutes a day | Going outside every morning |Writing in a journal

Exercising 3x a week | Drinking more water | Drawing or creating something

Practicing an instrument | Doing one kind thing a day

- *My Habit:*

____

____

- *Why This One:*

____

____

My Habit Plan

- *Complete this sentence to make your habit automatic:*

After I _________________________ **every day, I will**

_________________________ **for** _________ **minutes.**

My 4-Week Sticker Chart

- *Put a checkmark or draw a star each day you do your habit:*

Week 1	Week 2	Week 3 and 4
M __ T __ W __ Th __ F __ Sa __ Su __	M __ T __ W __ Th __ F __ Sa __ Su __	Days 15-28: [ ] [ ] [ ] [ ] [ ] [ ] [ ] [ ] [ ] [ ] [ ] [ ] [ ] [ ] [ ] [ ] [ ]

My 4-Week Sticker Chart

- *Put a checkmark or draw a star each day you do your habit:*

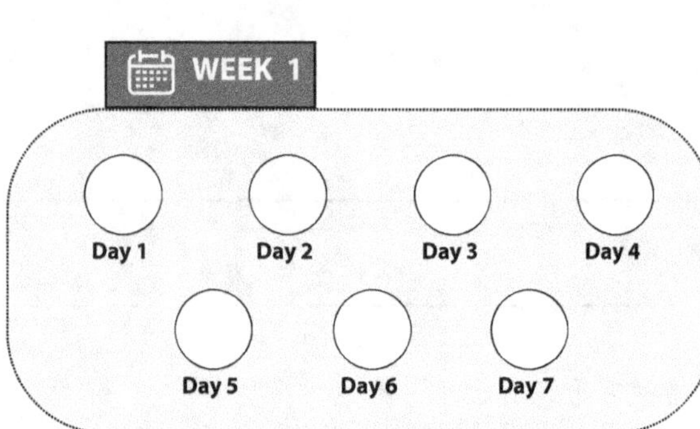

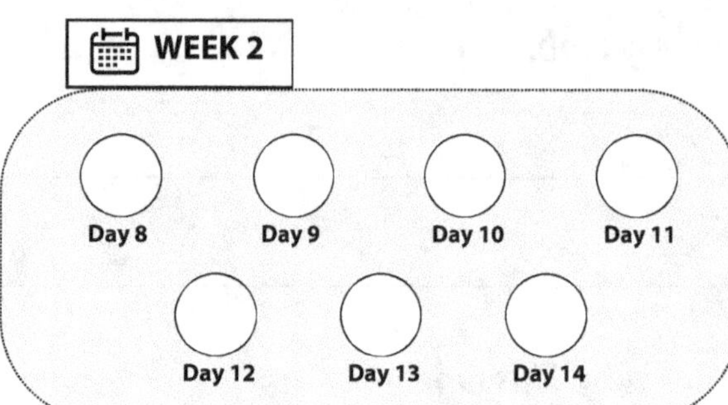

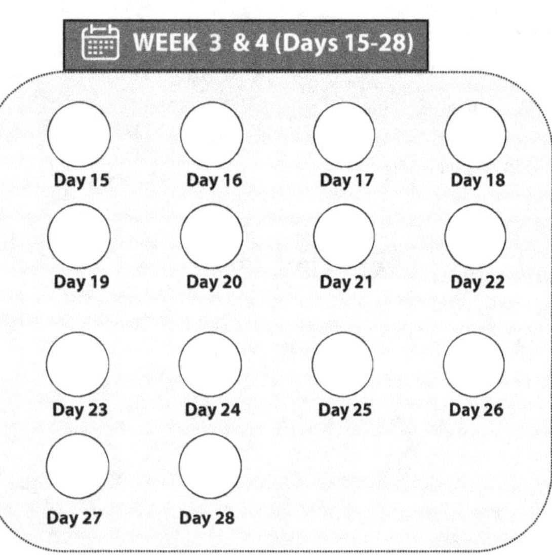

LOOKING BACK AT MY SUMMER

This exercise has two parts. Fill out Part 1 RIGHT NOW at the start of summer. Then come back and fill out Part 2 during the last week of summer. It is like writing a letter to your future self!

Part 1: Fill Out NOW - My Summer Hopes

- *What are the three things you most hope will happen this summer?*

1.

____

____

2.

____

____

3.

____

____

Part 2: Fill Out at END of Summer - What Actually Happened

I hoped this would happen:	What Actually Happened
Hope 1:	
Hope 2:	
Hope 3:	

Part 2 Continued: My Summer in 3 Words

- *At the end of summer, write three words that describe your summer:*

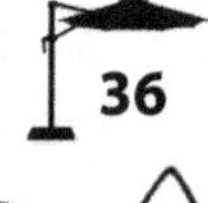

CHAPTER 3

LOOK AROUND

The World Beyond You

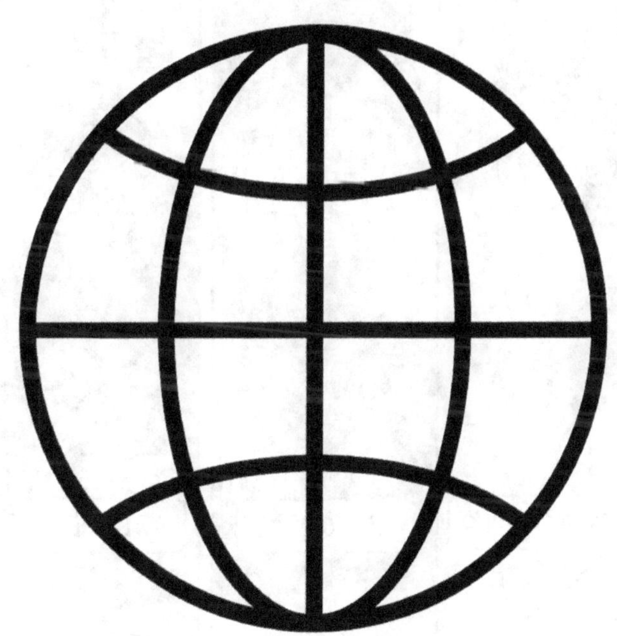

Social awareness means paying attention to the people around you - not just yourself. It means noticing how others feel, understanding that everyone has a different life, and caring about your community.

These exercises will help you see the world with kinder, more curious eyes.

NOT EVERY SUMMER
LOOKS THE SAME

Your summer might look really different from your friend's summer, your neighbor's summer, or a kid you don't even know on the other side of town. That is important to think about.

Different Kinds of Summers

- *List 5 ways that summers can look different for different kids your age:*

1. ____

2. ____

3. ____

4. ____

5. ____

Think About a Friend

- *Think about someone whose summer looks VERY different from yours. You don't have to write their name. What do you think their summer is like?*

____

____

____

____

- *What is something hard they might be dealing with that you do not have to worry about?*

____

____

What Can I Do?

- *Knowing that others have different summers, what is one way you could be kind or understanding this summer?*

EXERCISE 3.2

UNDERSTANDING OTHERS

Empathy is the superpower of understanding how someone else feels - even if you have never been in their exact situation. You don't have to go through the same thing to understand it.

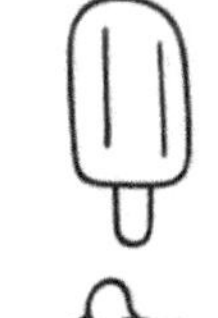

The Empathy Challenge

Imagine you are this person...	What might they be feeling?	What would help them feel better?
A friend who has to work all summer to help their family		
A kid who just moved to a new town right before summer		
A classmate whose parents are going through a divorce		
A friend who did not get invited to the same camp as everyone else		

Empathy in Real Life

- *Has someone ever shown real empathy toward you? What did they do and how did it make you feel?*

____

____

____

____

HOW CAN I HELP?

You do not have to be a grown-up to make a difference. Even tweens can do things that help their community, their neighborhood, or the people right around them. And it actually feels really good.

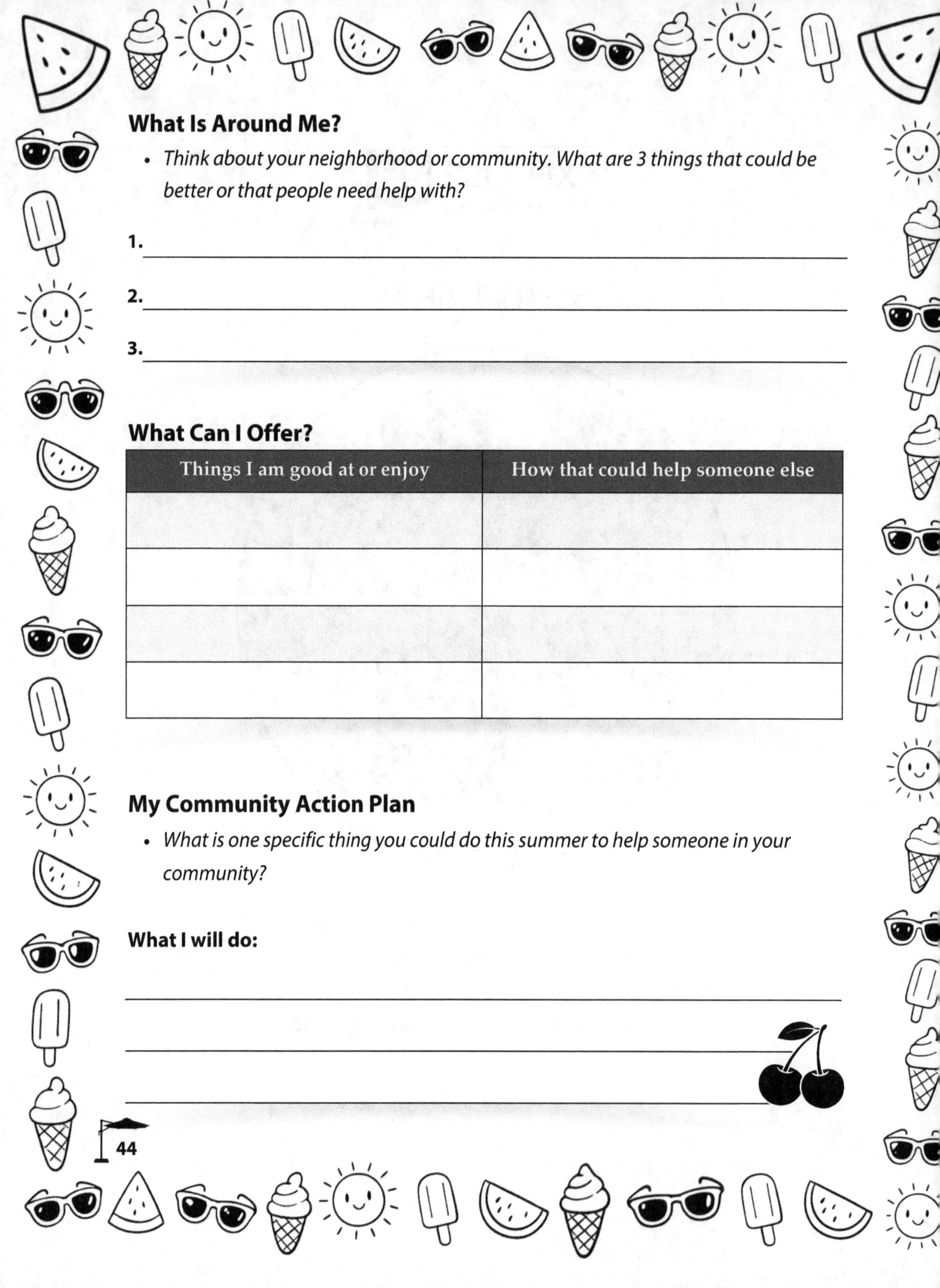

What Is Around Me?

- *Think about your neighborhood or community. What are 3 things that could be better or that people need help with?*

1. ____

2. ____

3. ____

What Can I Offer?

Things I am good at or enjoy	How that could help someone else

My Community Action Plan

- *What is one specific thing you could do this summer to help someone in your community?*

What I will do:

____

____

____

When I will do it:

____

____

____

Who it will help:

____

____

____

EXERCISE 3.4

SUMMER AROUND THE WORLD

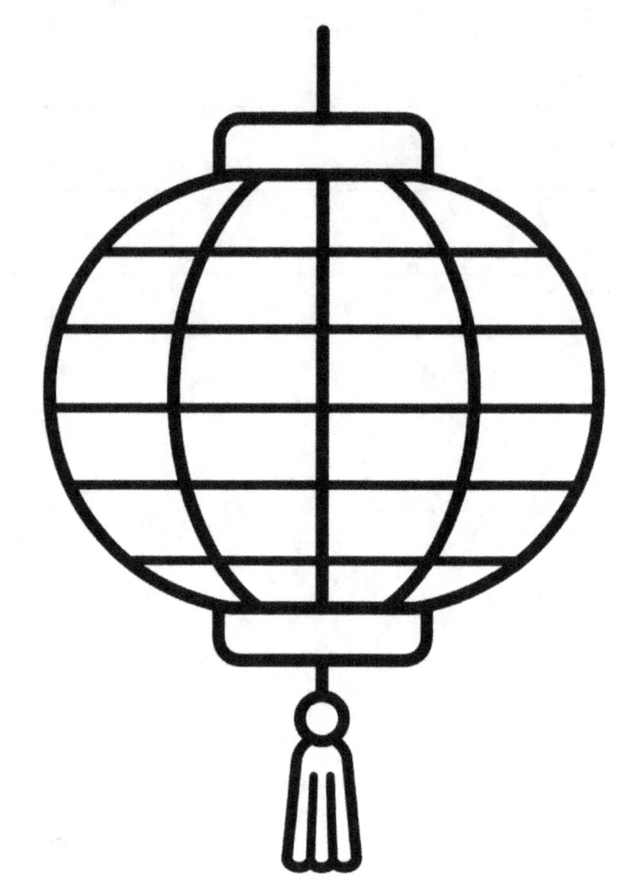

Did you know that summer looks completely different depending on where you are in the world? Some countries do not even have the same seasons! And every culture has its own special summer traditions, holidays, and celebrations.

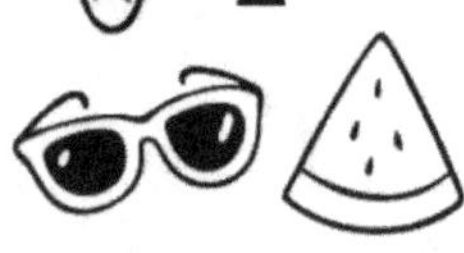

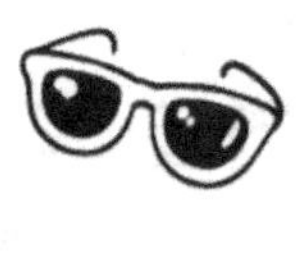

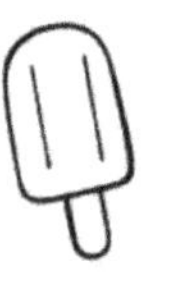

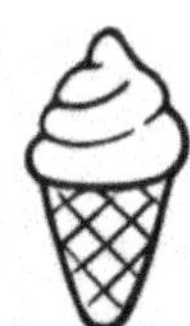

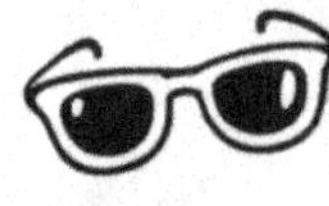

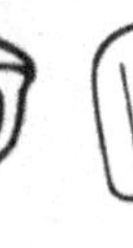

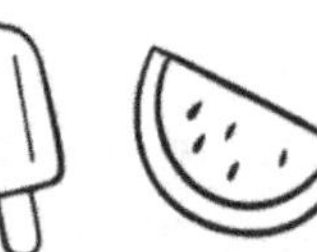

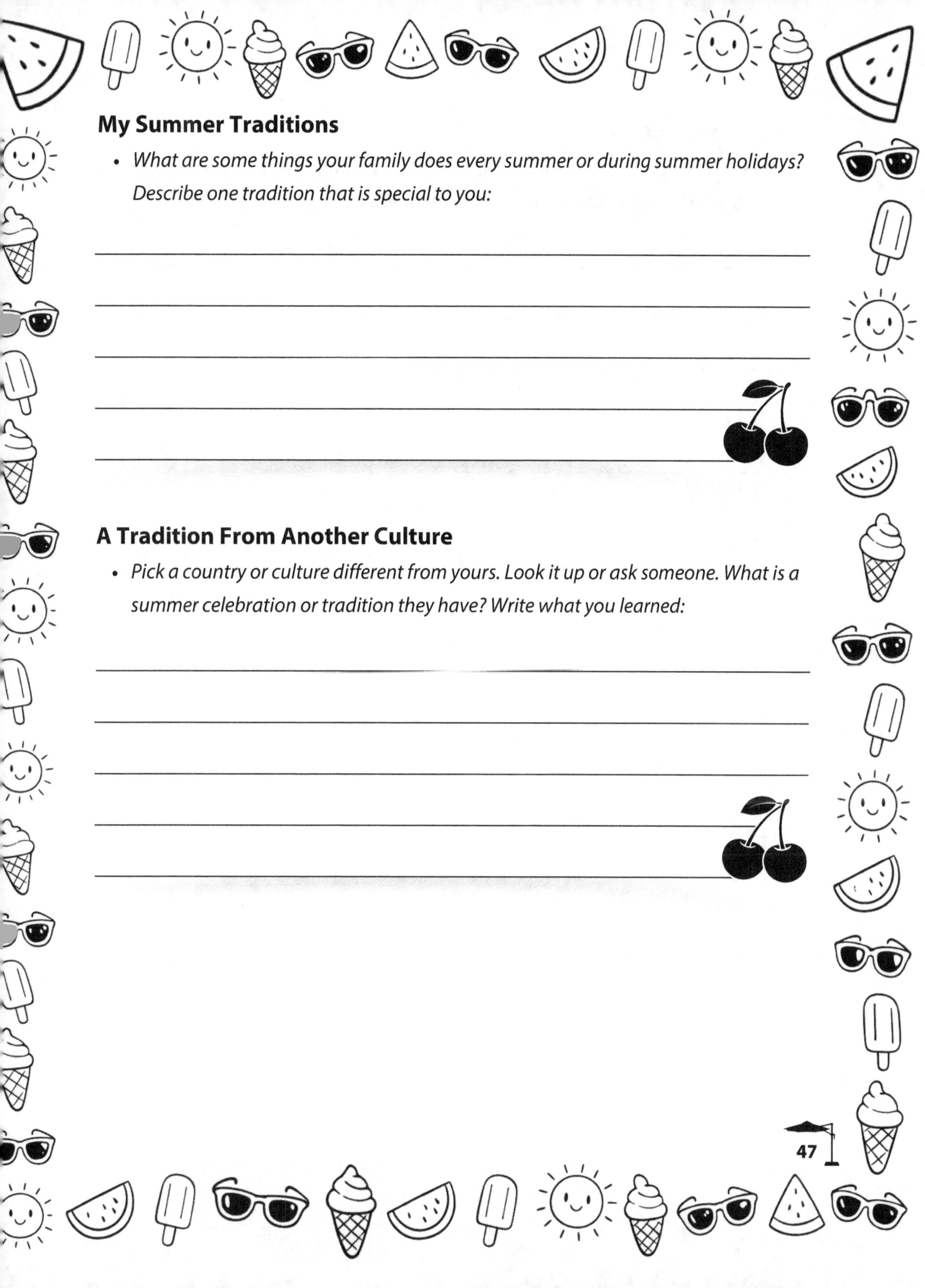

My Summer Traditions

- *What are some things your family does every summer or during summer holidays? Describe one tradition that is special to you:*

____

____

____

____

A Tradition From Another Culture

- *Pick a country or culture different from yours. Look it up or ask someone. What is a summer celebration or tradition they have? Write what you learned:*

____

____

____

____

What I Think Is Cool

- *What is something about another culture's summer traditions that you think is really interesting or that you wish your family did?*

____

____

____

____

BEING THERE FOR A FRIEND

Summers are not always fun for everyone. Sometimes a friend might be going through something hard - family stuff, feeling lonely, moving away, or just having a rough time. A good friend knows how to show up.

What Does Good Support Look Like?

What HELPS when a friend is struggling	What DOESN'T HELP (even when you mean well)
Just listening without trying to fix it	Saying *'just cheer up'* or *'it's not a big deal'*
Checking in on them without making it weird	Telling everyone else what they told you
Including them even when they seem quiet	Disappearing when things get heavy

Reaching Out

- *Is there a friend who might be having a hard summer? You don't have to write their name. What is ONE thing you could do to show them you care?*

____

____

____

____

Remember:

You do not have to fix everything. Sometimes just showing up and saying 'I'm here' is the most powerful thing you can do.

READING THE ROOM

Reading the room means noticing the mood or vibe of a place or group without anyone having to tell you. It is a really useful skill - especially in summer when you are in lots of different social situations.

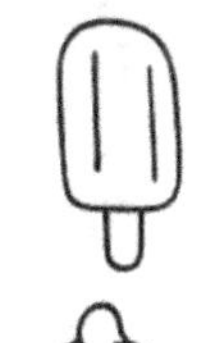

What Would You Notice?

The Situation	What signals would you look for?	How would you respond?
You walk into a friend's house and everyone seems really quiet and tense		
Your friend says *'I'm fine'* but looks like they've been crying		
A new kid shows up at your summer program and looks lost and nervous		

What Signals Do YOU Give Off?

- *When you are upset, bored, or feeling left out - what do you do that other people might notice, even if you don't say anything?*

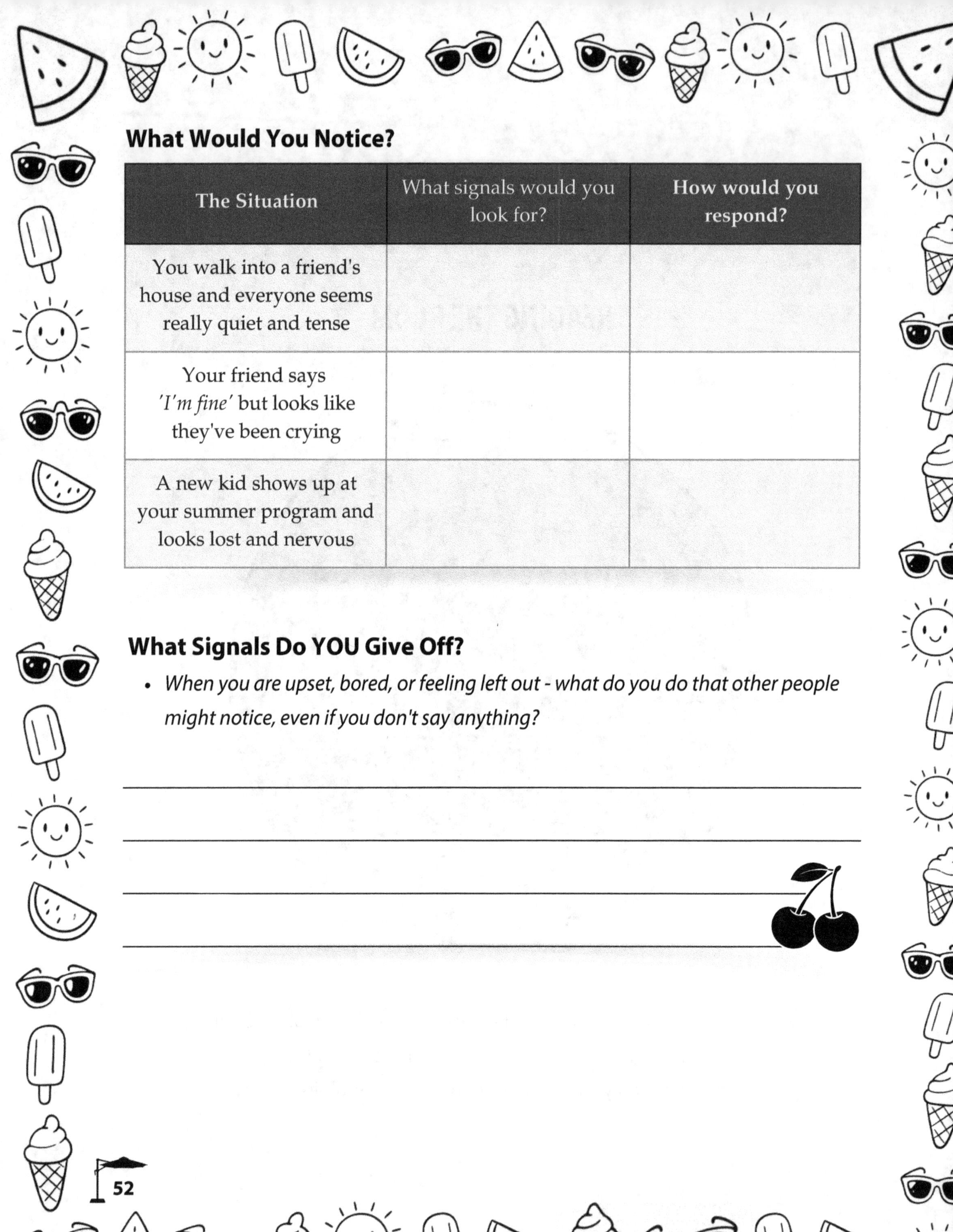

- *Why is it useful to know this about yourself?*

____

____

____

____

____

EXERCISE 3.7

INCLUDING EVERYONE

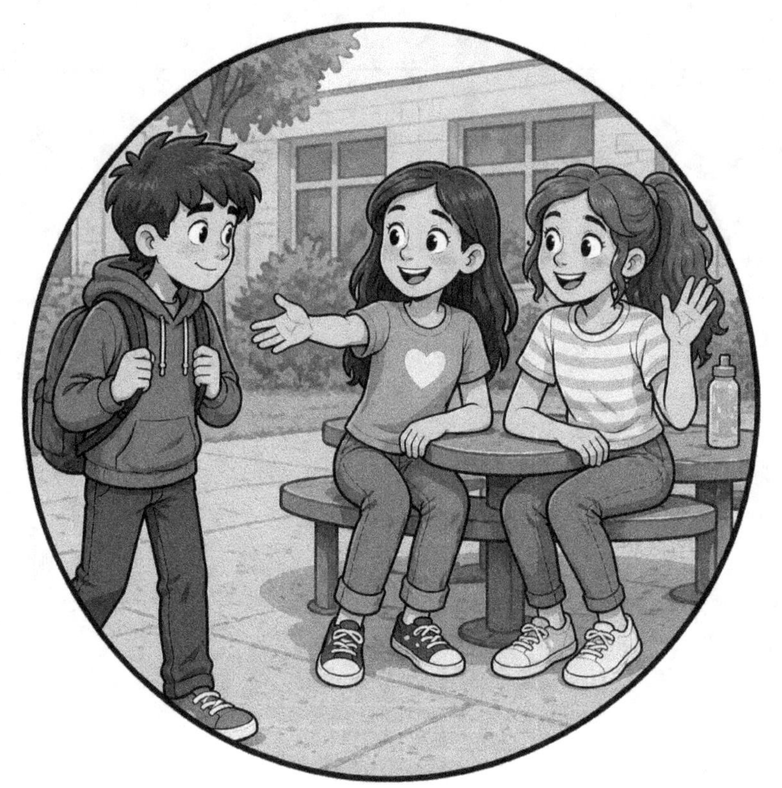

It feels awful to be left out. Most of us have felt that way at some point. This exercise is about being the kind of person who notices when someone is on the outside - and does something about it.

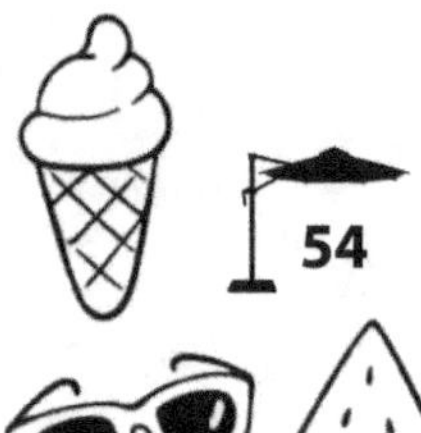

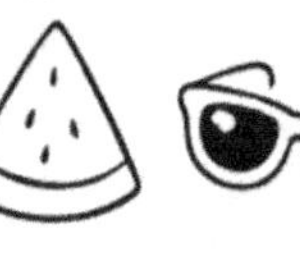

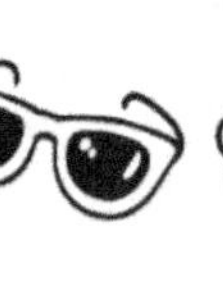

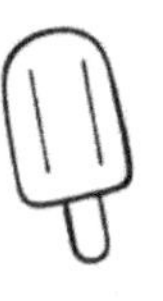

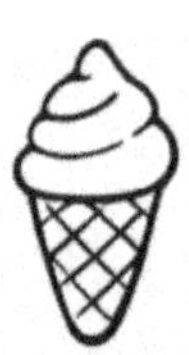

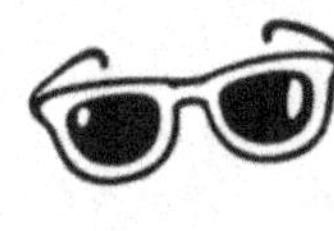

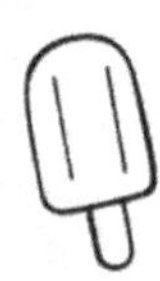

Left Out Moments

- *Think about a time when YOU felt left out. What happened and how did it feel?*

____

____

____

Who Gets Left Out in My World?

- *Think about your group of friends or your summer program. Is there anyone who tends to be left out of plans or conversations? What is one thing you could do to include them?*

____

____

____

Planning With Everyone in Mind

Before you make plans this summer, try asking yourself these questions:

- *Is there anyone who might feel left out of this plan?*
- *Can everyone afford to do this, or do we need a cheaper option?*
- *Does the timing work for people who have activities or jobs?*
- *Will everyone feel comfortable and welcome there?*

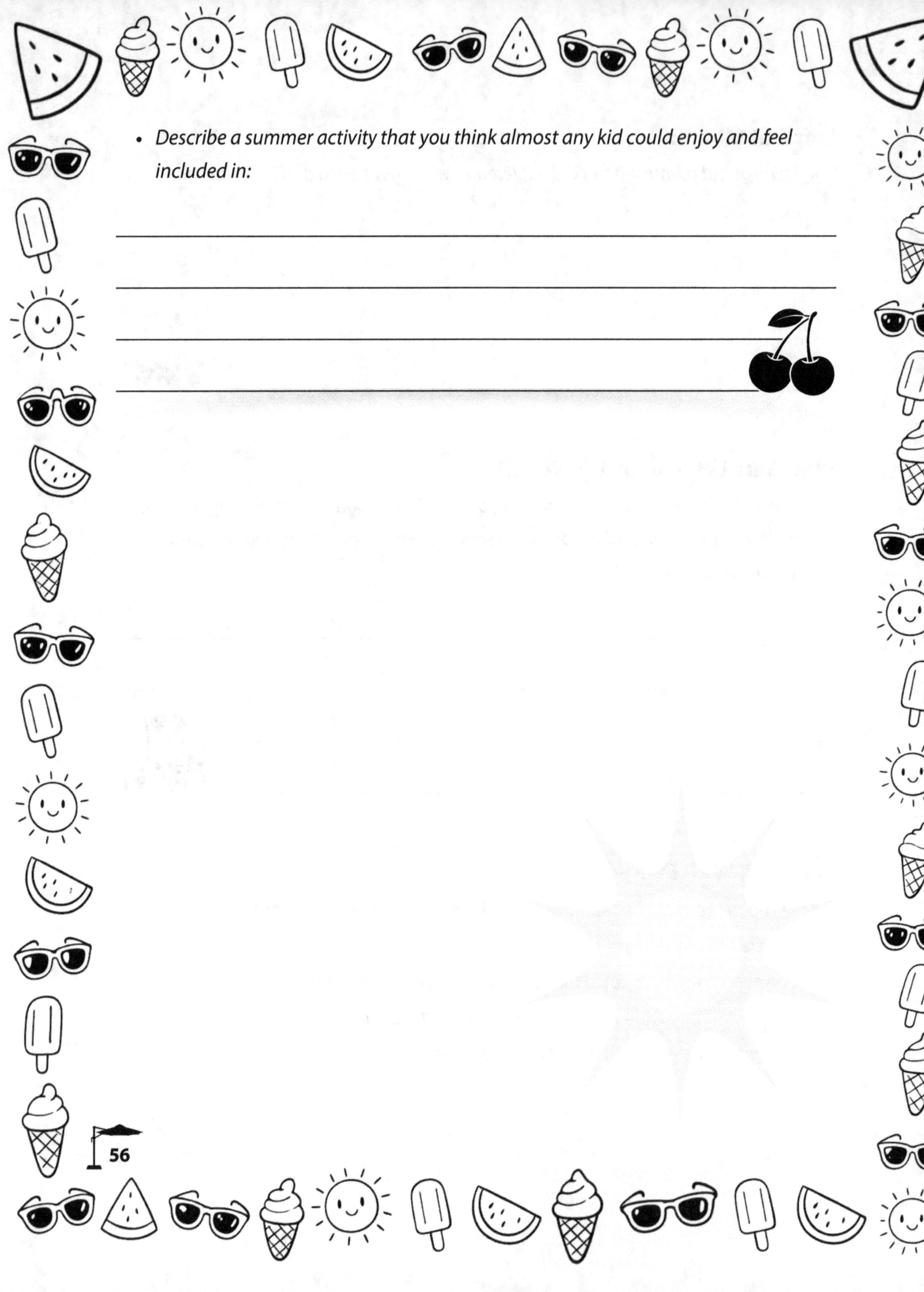

- *Describe a summer activity that you think almost any kid could enjoy and feel included in:*

CHAPTER 4

Your People

Friendships and Family This Summer

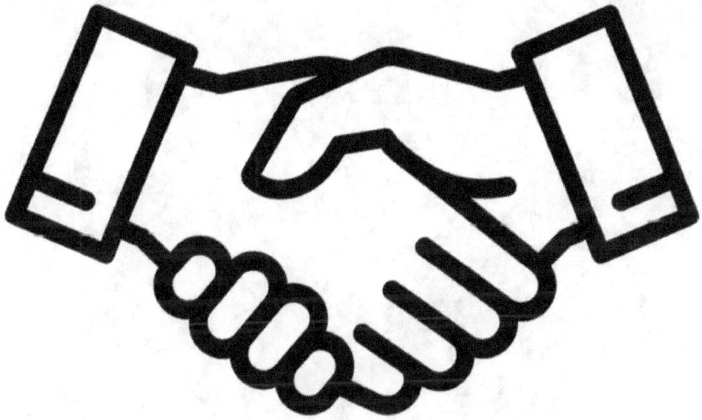

Summer changes your relationships. You see some friends more. Some drift away. You spend more time with family. And sometimes there is drama you were not expecting.

These exercises will help you handle all of it - the good parts AND the tricky parts.

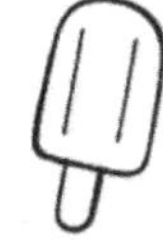

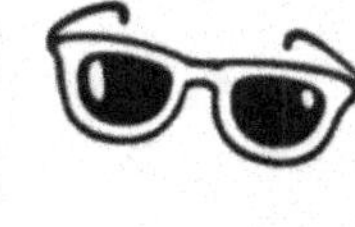

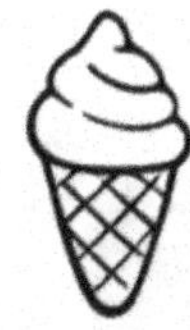

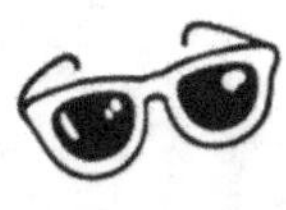

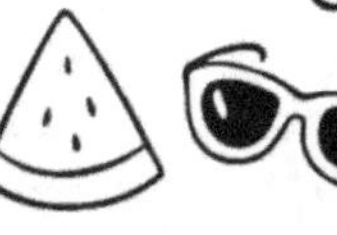

KEEPING FRIENDSHIPS GOING

During the school year, you see your friends almost every day without even trying. Summer takes that away. Some friendships stay strong. Others get a little lost. The difference is usually effort.

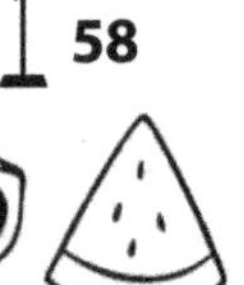

My Friendship Map

Friend's Name (or initials)	What might make staying connected hard this summer?

Ways to Stay Connected

- *List 5 ways to keep a friendship going even when you can't see each other in person:*

1.____

2.____

3.____

4.____

5.____

My Plan for One Important Friendship

- *Pick one friendship you want to make sure stays strong this summer. What is your specific plan?*

The friend I'm thinking of:

____

My plan:

____

____

____

____

HANDLING FRIEND DRAMA

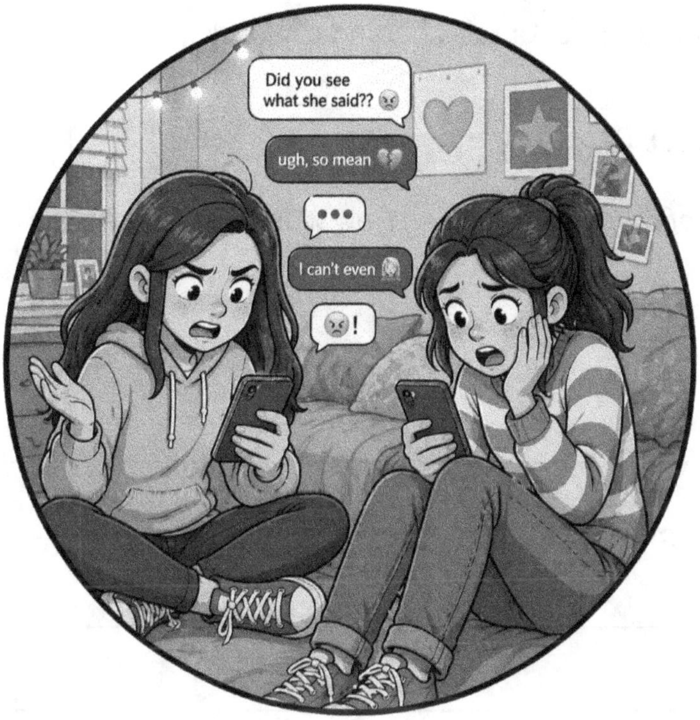

Summer friend drama is real. You have more free time, more group texts, more unstructured hangouts - and more chances for things to go sideways. The good news is that how you handle it is completely in your control.

Types of Friend Drama

Check the ones you have experienced or think might happen this summer:

- Someone leaves me out of plans
- A group chat blows up over something small
- Two friends are fighting and I'm caught in the middle
- A friend says something that hurts my feelings
- I say something that hurts a friend's feelings
- Someone starts a rumor or talks behind my back

My Drama-Free Response Plan

- *Pick one type of drama from the list. How would you handle it in a way you'd be proud of?*

Drama type:

____

- **My response plan:**

____

____

____

The Friendship Rule I Live By

- *What is YOUR personal rule for how you treat friends?* Write it here:

____

____

____

____

____

EXERCISE 4.3

MORE FAMILY TIME

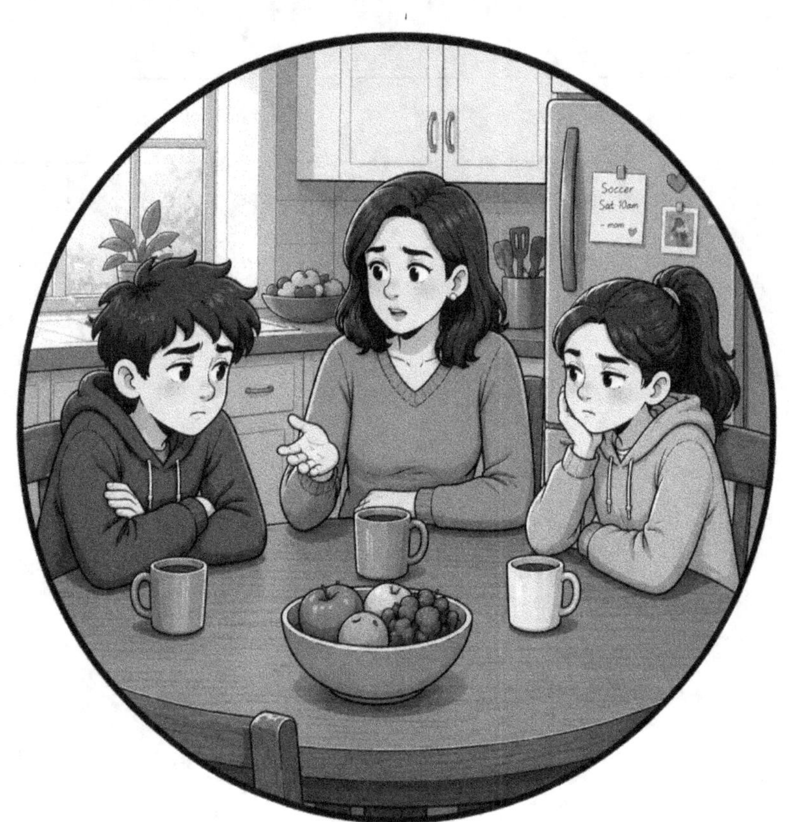

Summer means more time at home. More family meals. More *'what are you doing?'* from parents. More sibling time whether you want it or not. That can be really great - or really frustrating. Usually both.

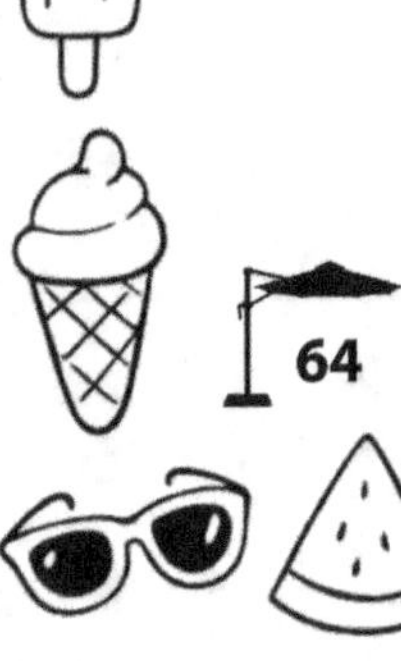

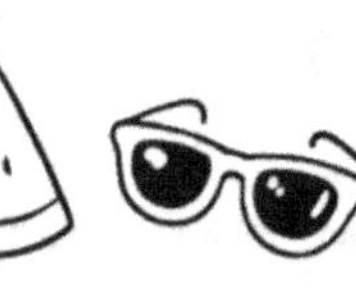

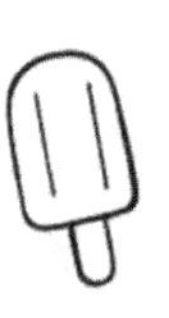

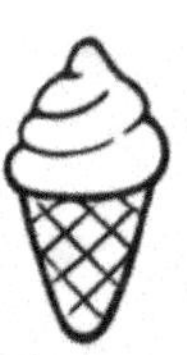

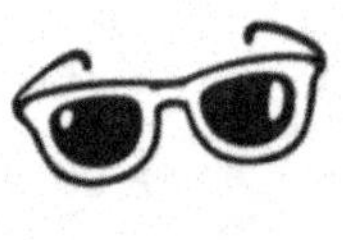

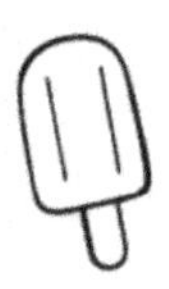

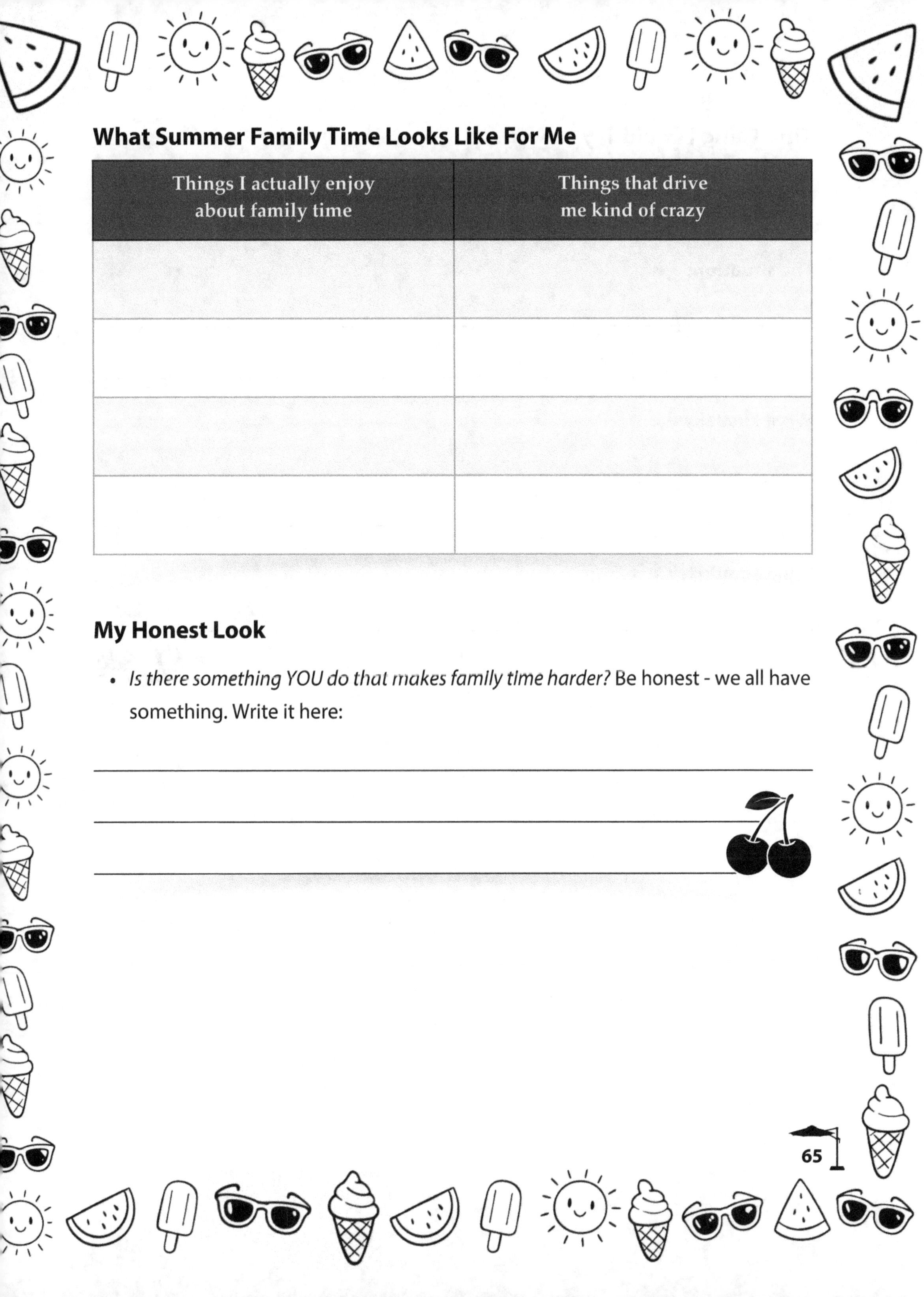

What Summer Family Time Looks Like For Me

Things I actually enjoy about family time	Things that drive me kind of crazy

My Honest Look

- *Is there something YOU do that makes family time harder?* Be honest - we all have something. Write it here:

____

____

____

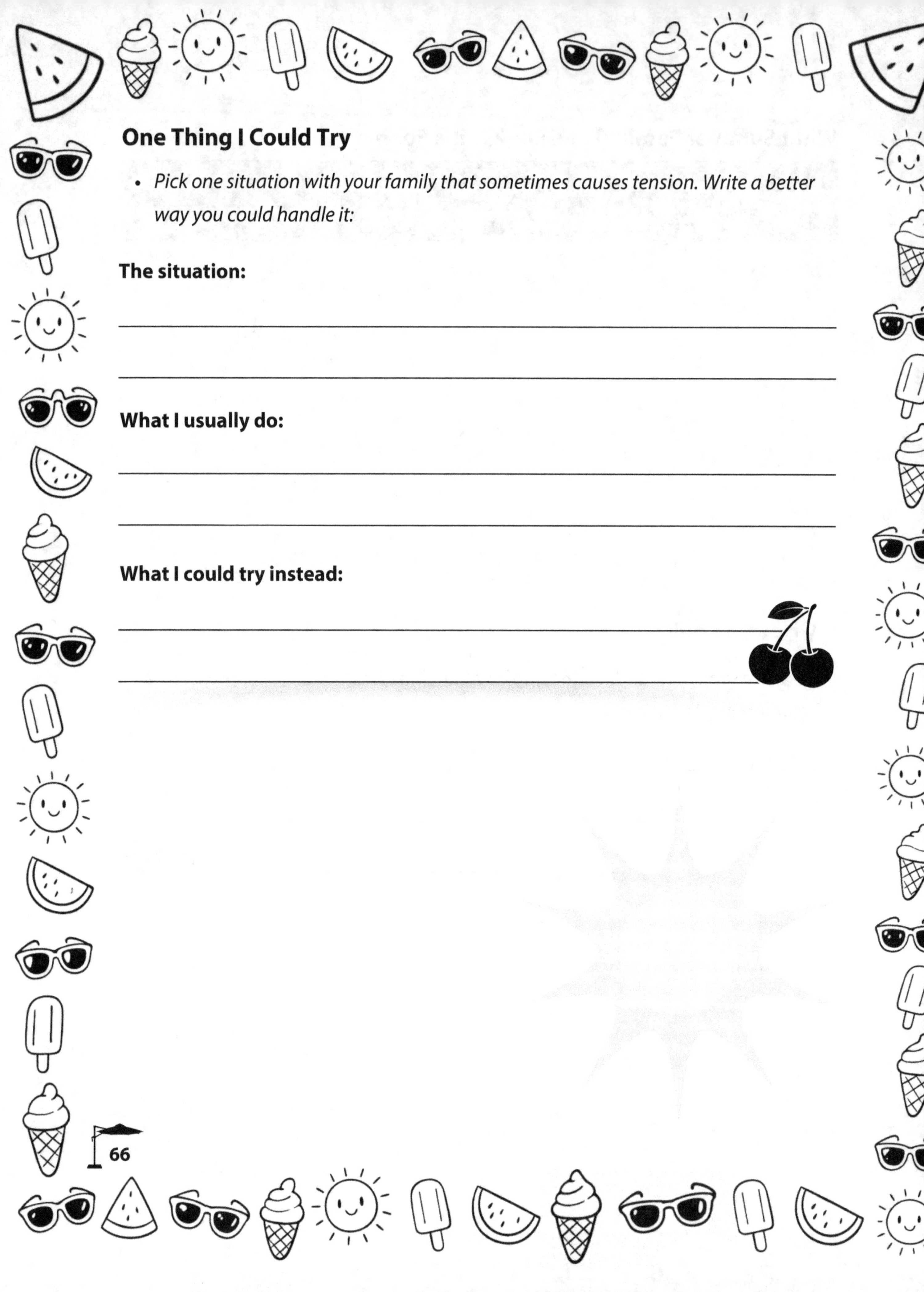

One Thing I Could Try

- *Pick one situation with your family that sometimes causes tension. Write a better way you could handle it:*

The situation:

____

____

What I usually do:

____

____

What I could try instead:

____

____

MAKING NEW FRIENDS

Summer can drop you into situations with brand new people - a camp, a program, a neighborhood, a team. Making friends from scratch can feel awkward. Here is how to make it a little easier.

How I Usually Make Friends

- *Think about how you have made friends in the past. What worked? What felt awkward?*

____

____

____

____

The First Move

- Starting a conversation is usually the hardest part. Here are some easy openers that actually work:

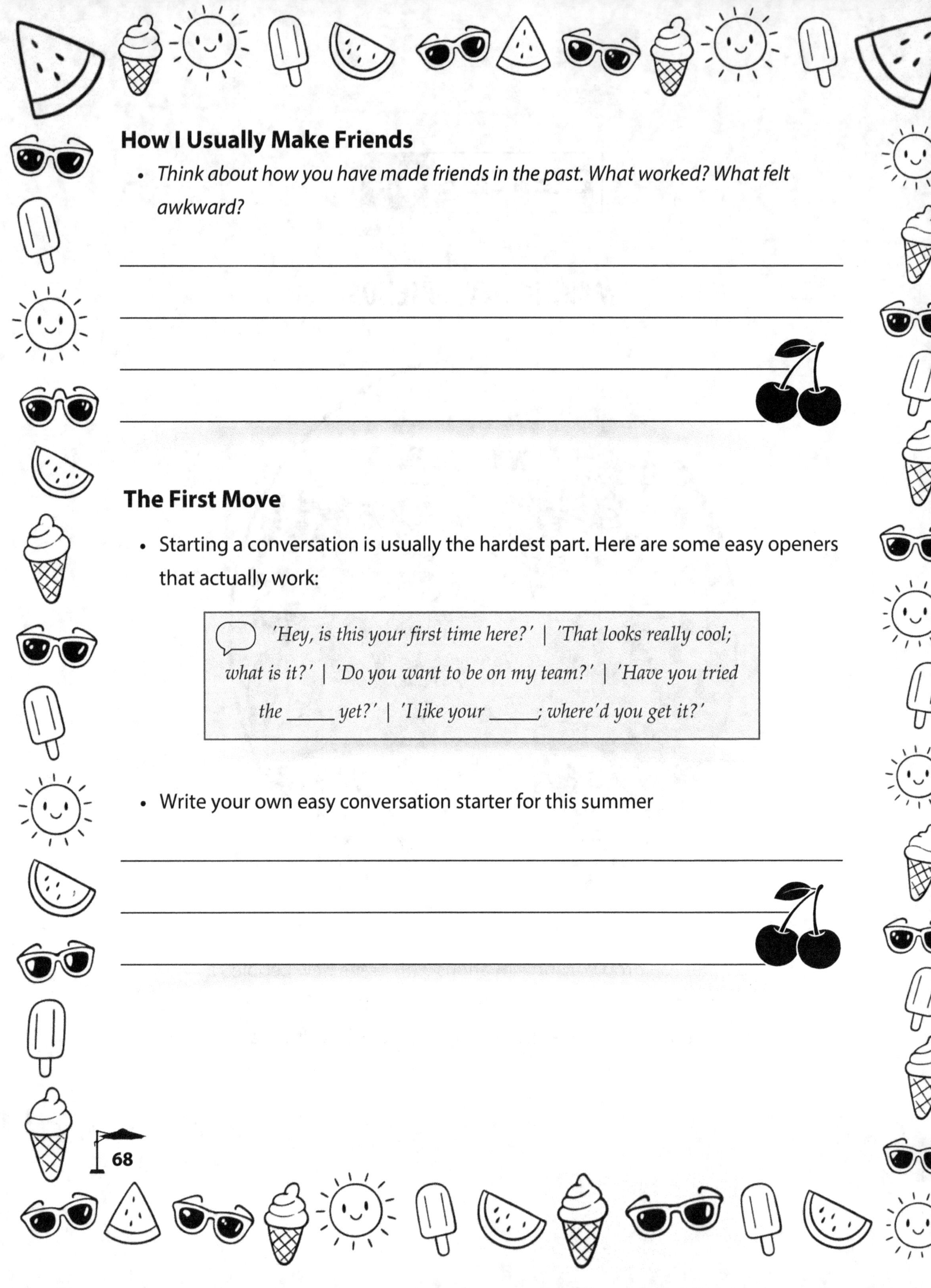

- Write your own easy conversation starter for this summer

____

____

____

Being a Good New Friend

- *Once you start talking to someone new, what makes them want to keep hanging out with you? What are the qualities of a person who is easy to befriend?*

____

____

____

____

____

EXERCISE 4.5

SAYING NO WITHOUT DRAMA

Saying no is a skill. And summer is full of situations where you might need it - plans you don't want to go to, things that don't feel right, or just times when you need a break. You are allowed to say no. Here is how to do it without making things weird.

When I Find It Hard to Say No

- *Circle all the situations where saying no feels difficult:*

> *When I don't want to hurt someone's feelings | When everyone else is saying yes | When I'm worried about being left out | When I feel pressured | When it's a close friend asking | When I don't have a good excuse*

- *What happens when you say yes to things you don't actually want to do?*

____

____

____

My 3 Go-To Ways to Say No

- *Write three ways to say no that are honest but kind - something you would actually say:*

1.____

____

2.____

____

3.____

____

EXERCISE 4.6

WHEN ARGUMENTS HAPPEN

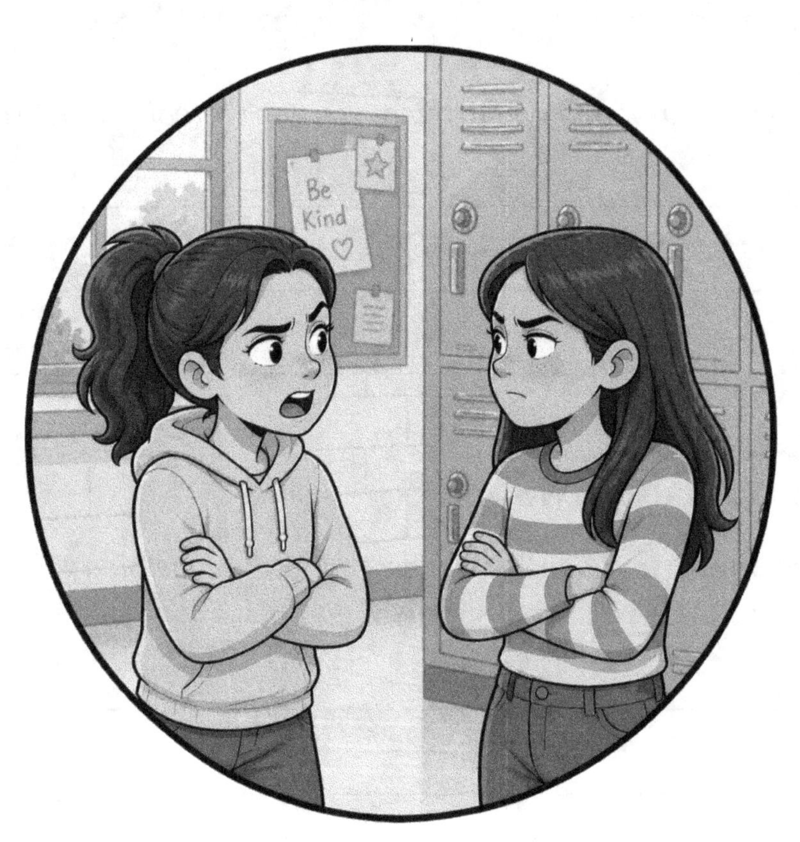

Arguments are part of every relationship. They happen with friends, siblings, parents, and pretty much everyone you are close to. The key is not to avoid all arguments - it is to handle them in a way that makes things BETTER instead of worse.

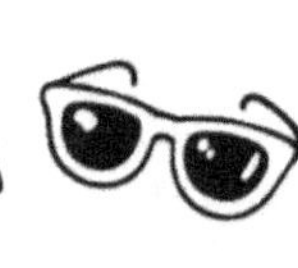

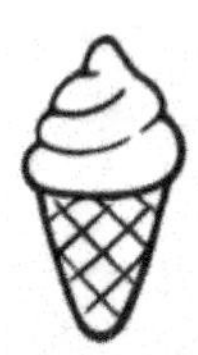

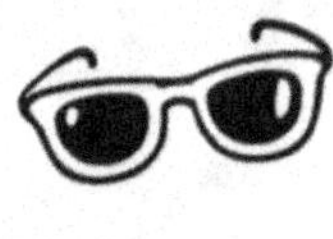

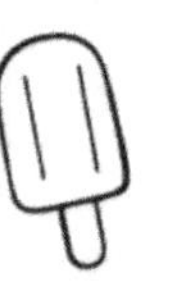

My Argument Style

- *When I get into an argument, I usually... (circle all that apply):*

  Go quiet and ignore everyone | Say stuff I don't mean | Storm off

  | Try to talk it out calmly | Cry | Get louder |

  Text about it instead of saying it in person | Let it fester for days

- *Is that working for you? What would you change about how you handle arguments?*

____

____

____

____

A Better Playbook

6. Take a breath—or take a break—before you respond.
7. Say what BOTHERED you, not what's wrong with the other person.
8. Listen to their side even if you disagree.
9. Try to find one thing you can agree on.
10. Let it actually be over when it's over - don't keep bringing it up.

- *Think of a recent argument. How could this approach have changed it?*

EXERCISE 4.7

WHEN WE HAVE
DIFFERENT SCHEDULES

In summer, everyone has different schedules. Your best
friend might be at camp for six weeks. Your cousin might
visit for a month. Your other friend might work. Life gets
messy - but friendships don't have to fall apart.

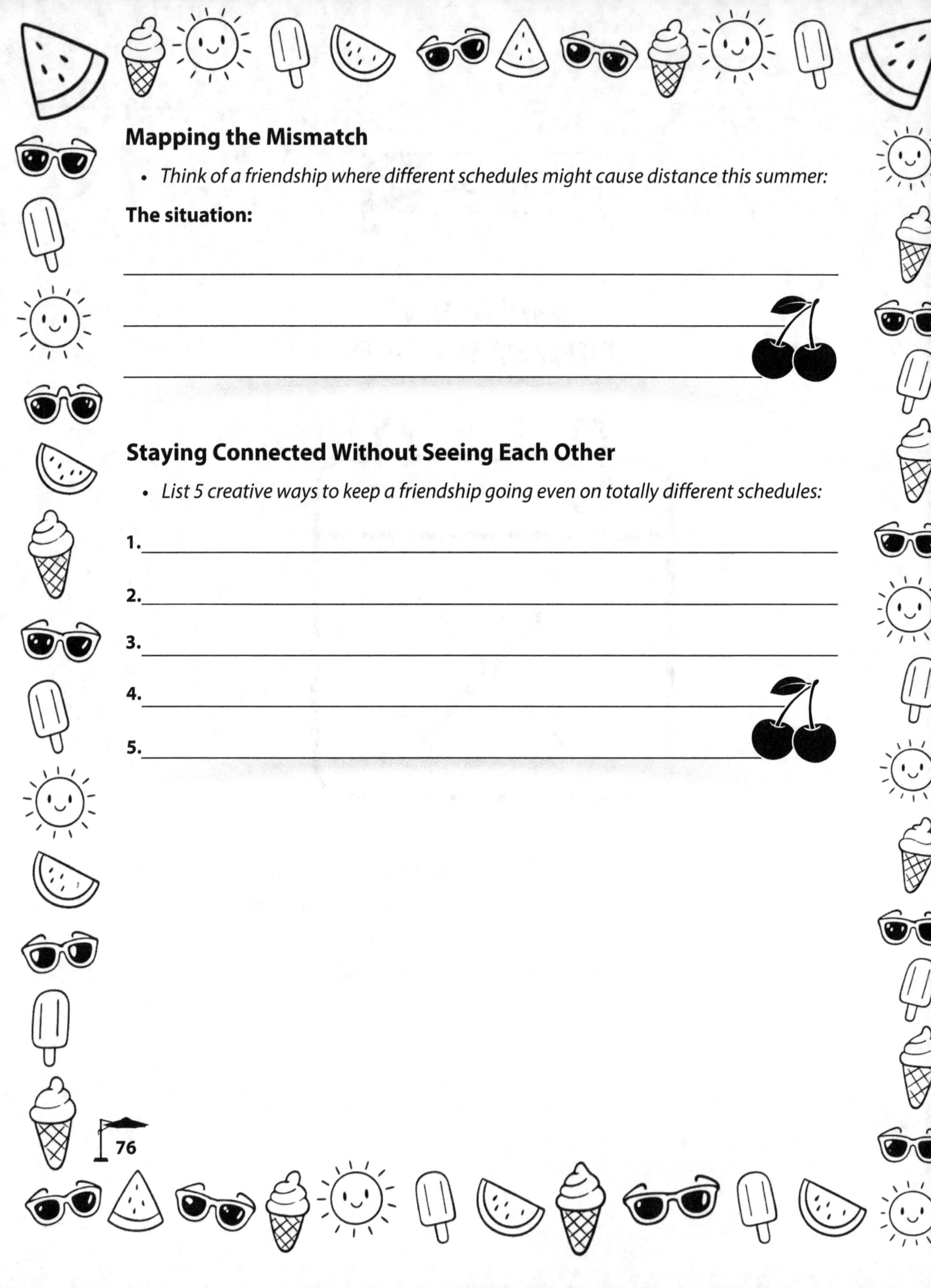

Mapping the Mismatch

- *Think of a friendship where different schedules might cause distance this summer:*

The situation:

____

____

____

Staying Connected Without Seeing Each Other

- *List 5 creative ways to keep a friendship going even on totally different schedules:*

1.____

2.____

3.____

4.____

5.____

My Realistic Plan

- *For that one friendship with mismatched schedules - what is a simple, realistic thing you can do to keep it going?*

____

____

____

____

____

CHAPTER 5

Smart Choices

Making Good Decisions All Summer Long

Summer gives you more freedom than almost any other time of year. More free time, more independence, more situations where YOU have to decide what to do. That is exciting - and it also means your choices matter more.

This chapter will help you think through the kinds of decisions you will actually face this summer—before they happen.

EXERCISE 5.1

SHOULD I DO IT?

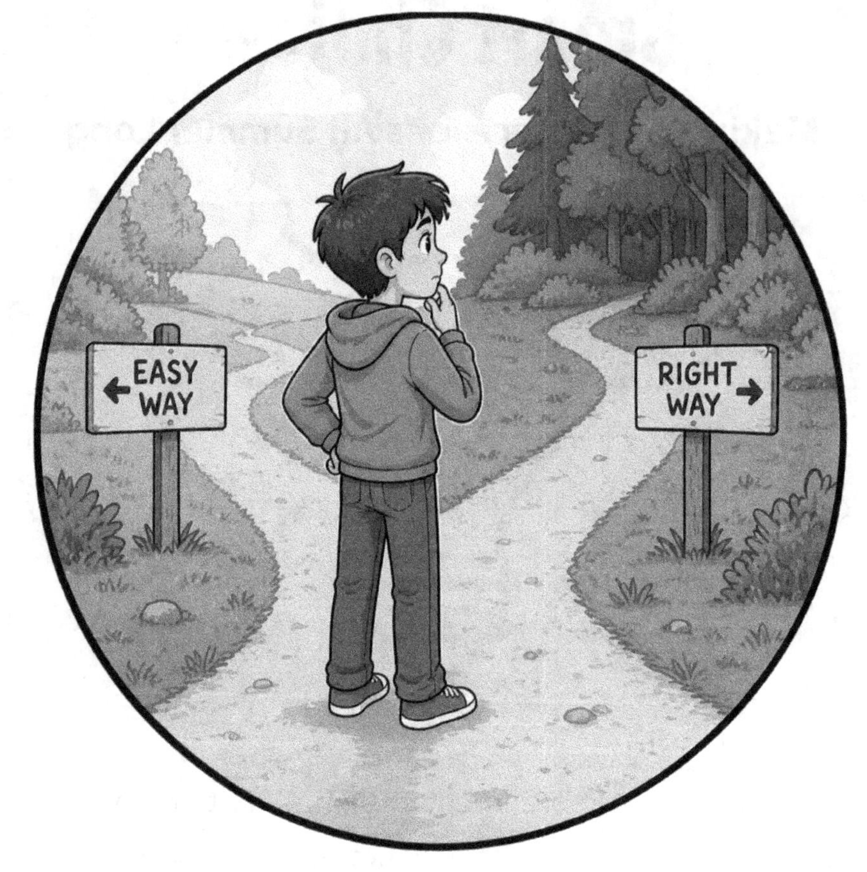

Before you say yes or no to something this summer, it helps to have a quick way to think it through. Here is a simple checklist you can use whenever a decision feels tricky.

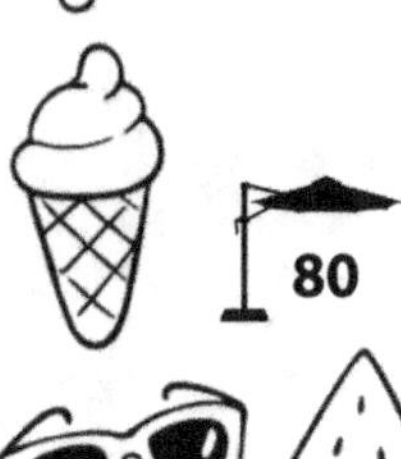

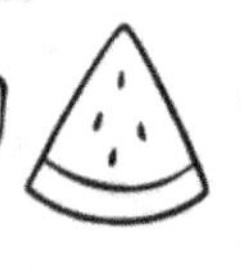

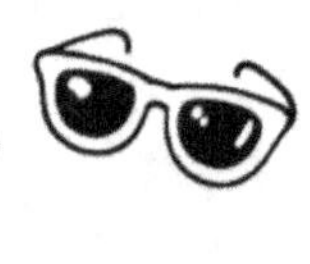

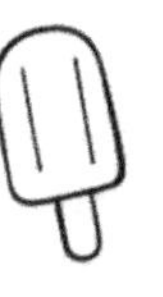

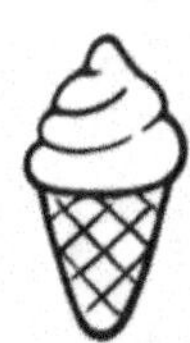

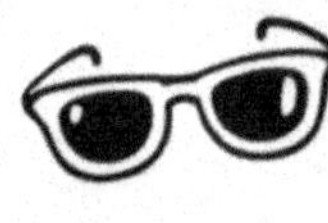

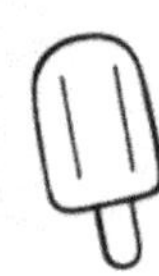

The Decision Checklist

Ask yourself this...	Your honest answer:
Will I feel proud of this tomorrow?	
Is anyone going to get hurt by this choice?	
Would I be okay if my parents/guardian found out?	
Am I doing this because I actually want to, or because of pressure?	
Does this match what I said I cared about in Chapter 1?	
What would my wisest friend tell me to do?	

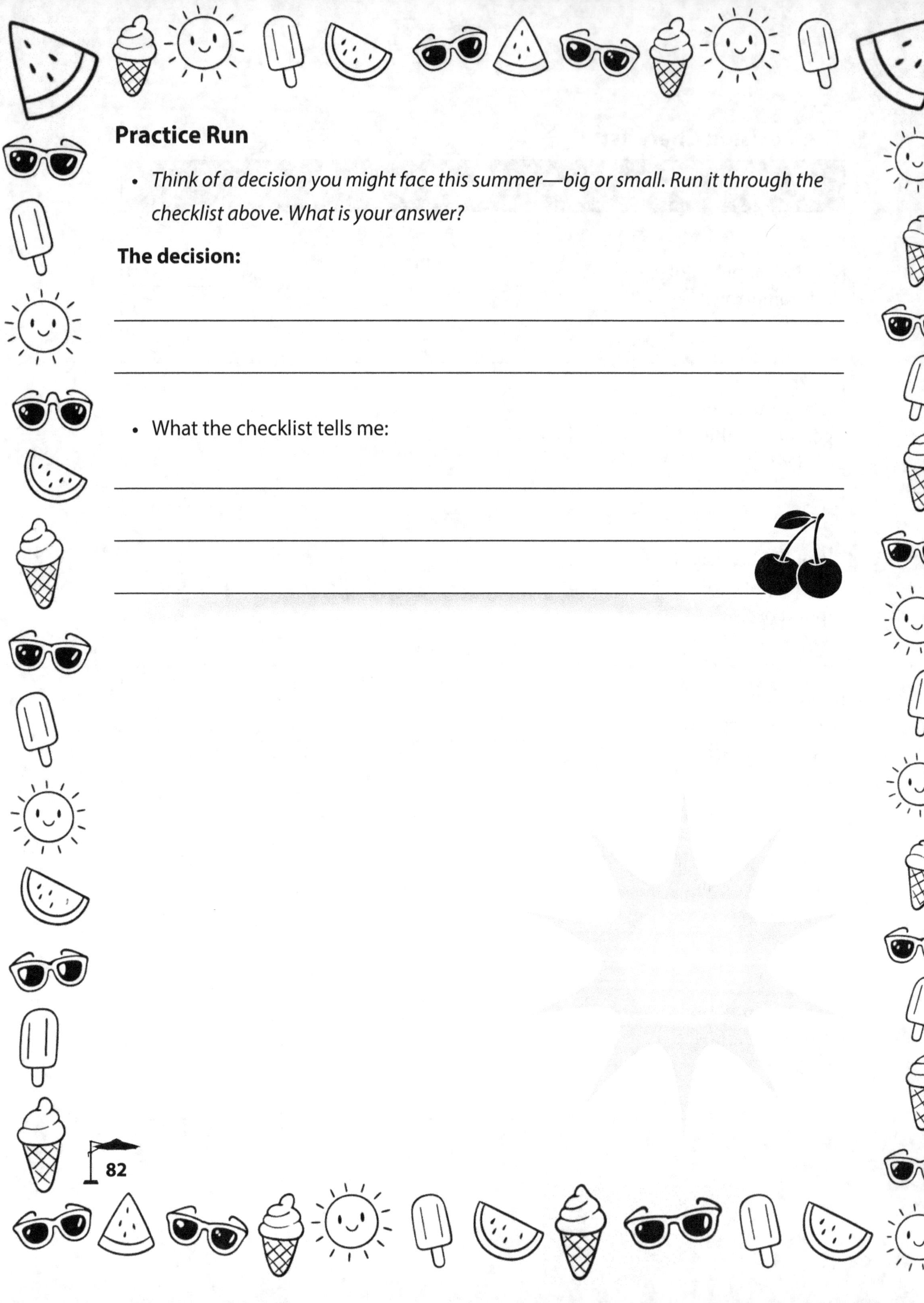

Practice Run

- *Think of a decision you might face this summer—big or small. Run it through the checklist above. What is your answer?*

The decision:

____

____

- What the checklist tells me:

____

____

____

EXERCISE 5.2

SAYING NO TO PEER PRESSURE

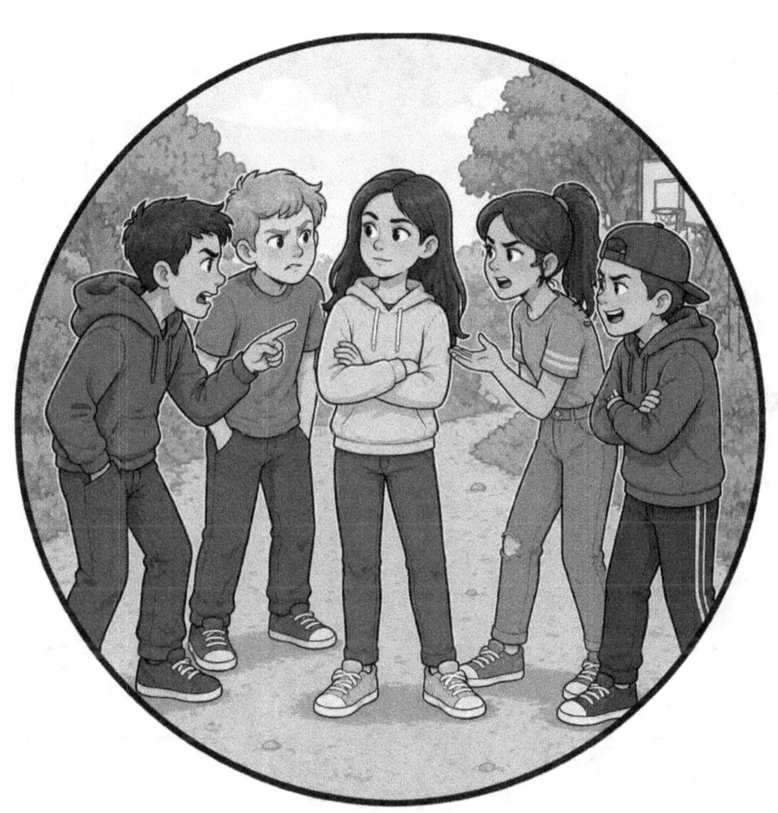

Peer pressure in summer is sneakier than it is during the school year. It is less about someone telling you what to do and more about just... everyone doing something and you feeling weird for NOT going along.

Types of Pressure

Type	What it sounds like	Why it's tricky
Direct	'Come on, just do it'	Someone is asking you straight up
Silent	No one says anything - everyone just does it	You feel weird being the only one who doesn't
Social	'Everyone else is doing it'	Makes you feel like you're missing out
Loyalty	'If you were really my friend you'd do it'	It feels like a test of the friendship

My No Toolkit

- *Write 3 ways to say no to pressure that sound like something YOU would actually say:*

1. _______________________________________

____

2. _______________________________________

____

3. _______________________________________

____

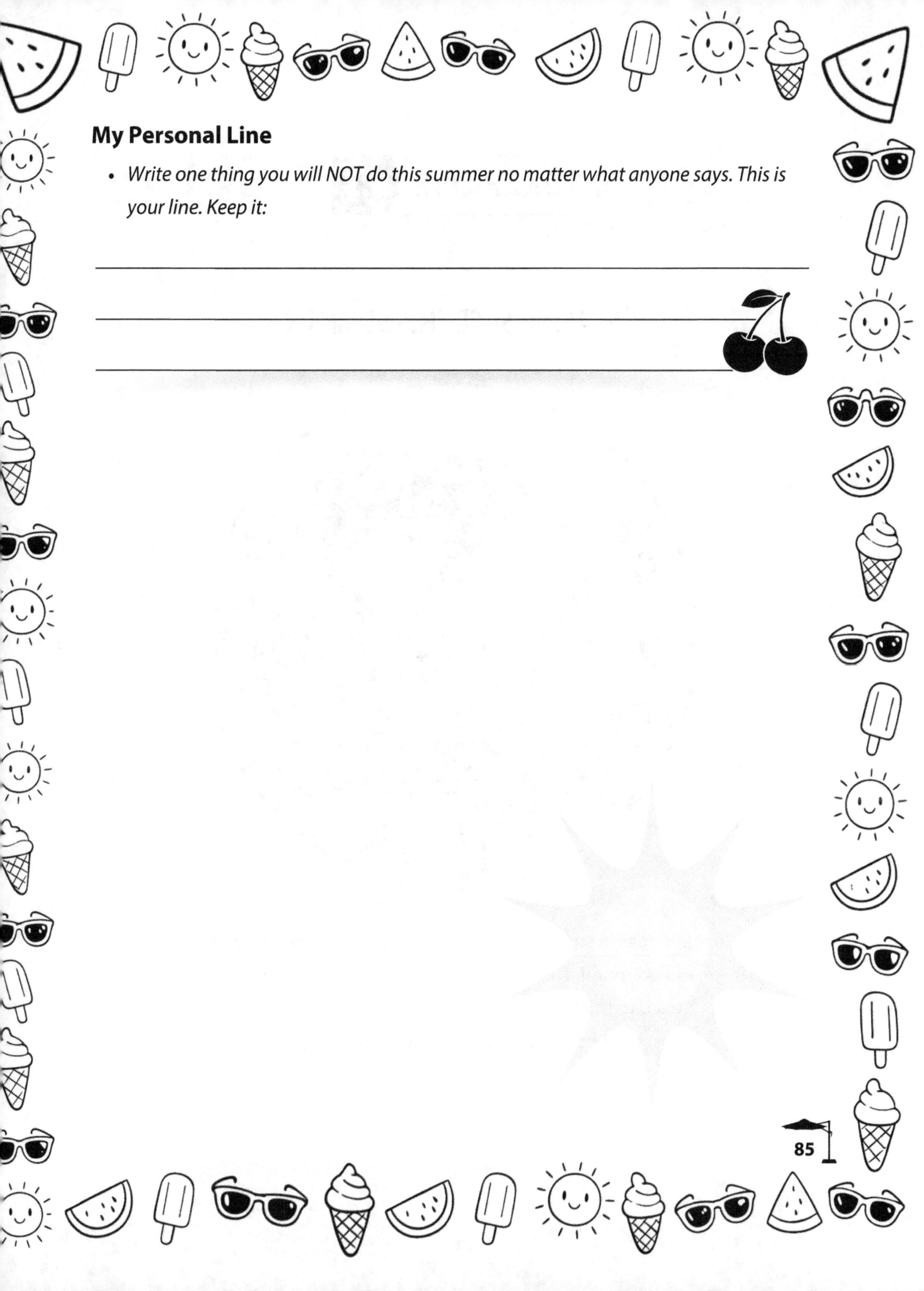

My Personal Line

- *Write one thing you will NOT do this summer no matter what anyone says. This is your line. Keep it:*

____

____

____

STAYING SAFE THIS SUMMER

Summer means more independence. More time without adults around. That is mostly great - but it also means you need to think ahead about some situations. This is not about being scared. It is about being prepared.

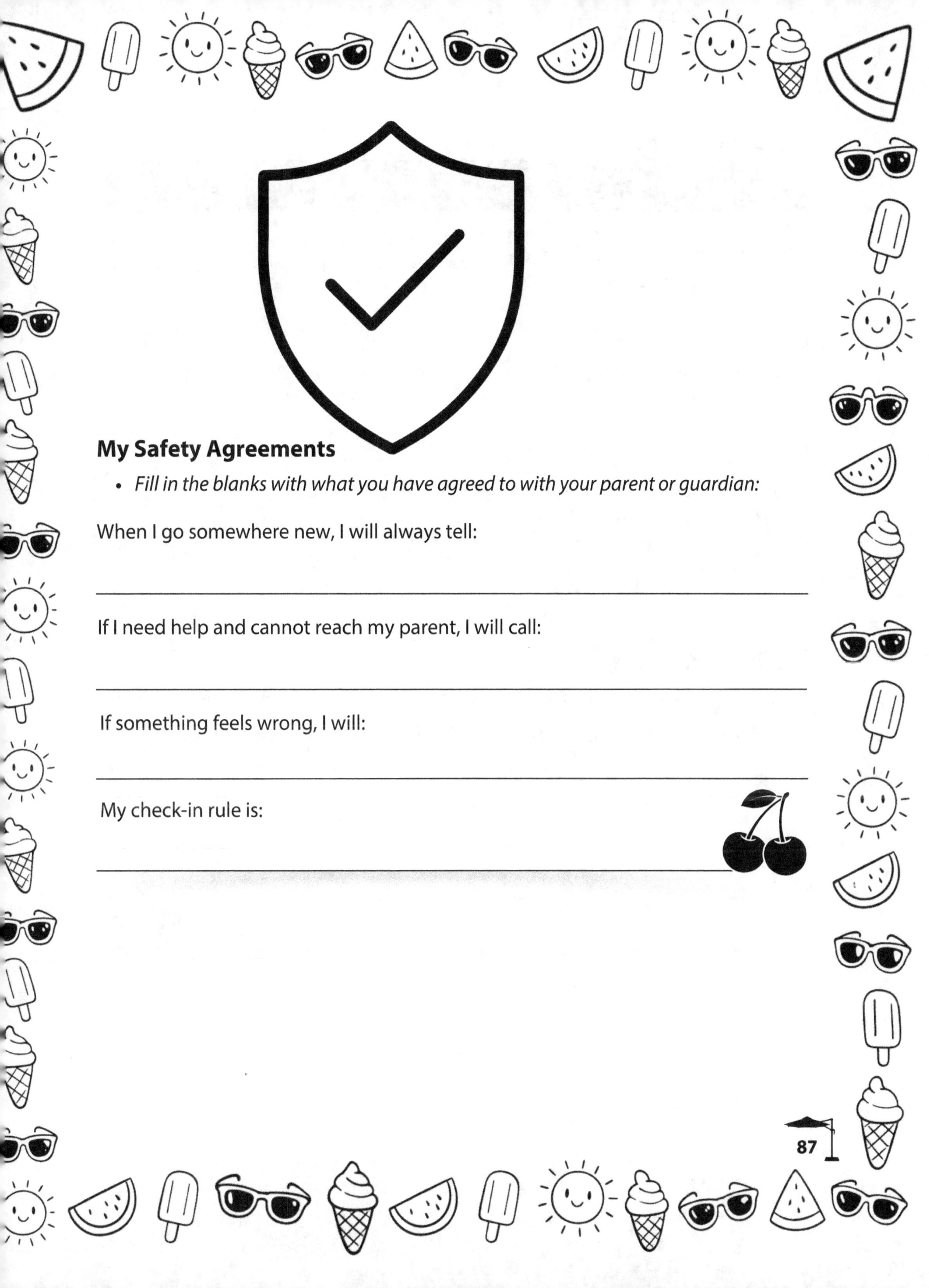

My Safety Agreements

- *Fill in the blanks with what you have agreed to with your parent or guardian:*

When I go somewhere new, I will always tell:

____

If I need help and cannot reach my parent, I will call:

____

If something feels wrong, I will:

____

My check-in rule is:

____

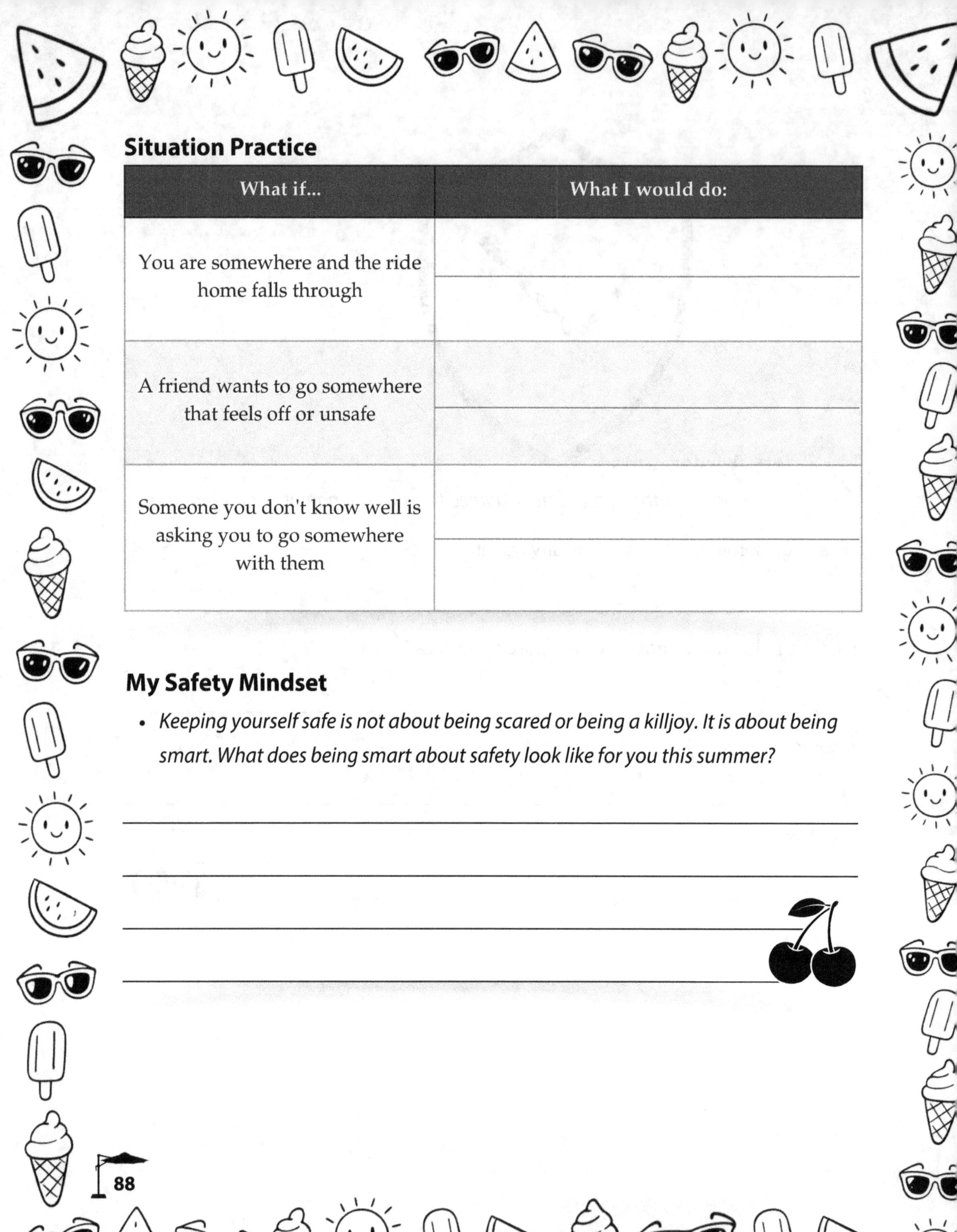

Situation Practice

What if...	What I would do:
You are somewhere and the ride home falls through	
A friend wants to go somewhere that feels off or unsafe	
Someone you don't know well is asking you to go somewhere with them	

My Safety Mindset

- *Keeping yourself safe is not about being scared or being a killjoy. It is about being smart. What does being smart about safety look like for you this summer?*

____

____

____

____

FOLLOWING THROUGH ON COMMITMENTS

A commitment is a promise - to yourself or someone else. This summer you might have commitments to a sports team, a job, a program, a volunteer role, or just plans with friends. How you handle those commitments says a lot about who you are.

My Summer Commitments

My Commitment	Am I Showing Up? Yes / Mostly / Not Really

The Follow-Through Check

Am I doing this?	My Rating (1-5)	What I Could Improve
Showing up on time		
Doing my best, not just the minimum		
Being reliable when people count on me		
Communicating when something comes up		

My Commitment Goal

- *What is one area where you want to be more reliable or responsible this summer?*

____

____

____

____

EXERCISE 5.5

TAKING CARE OF MY BODY AND MIND

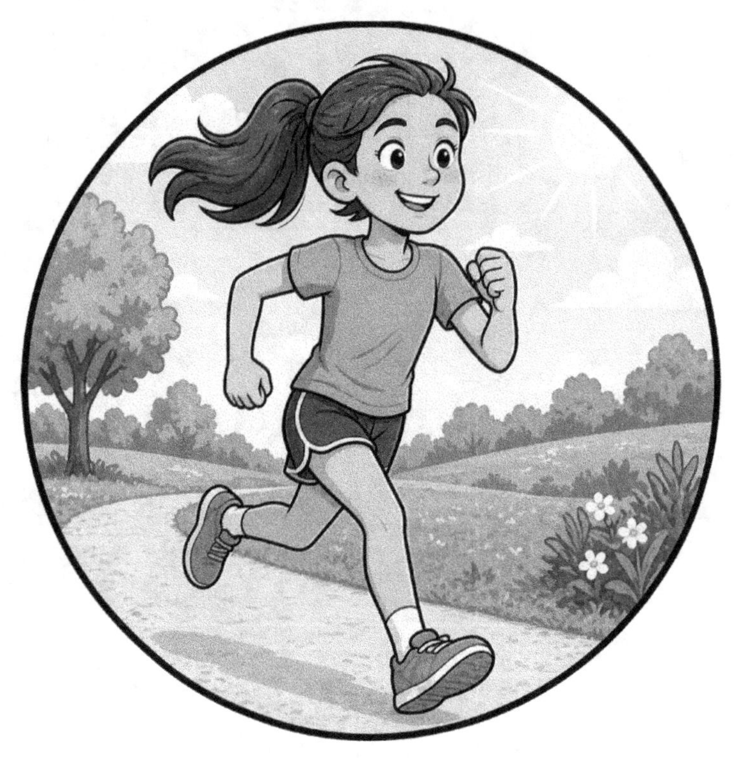

How you take care of yourself this summer affects EVERYTHING - your mood, your energy, your relationships, and how much you enjoy the next three months. The good news is that small changes make a huge difference.

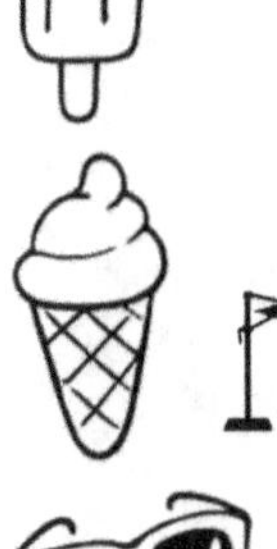

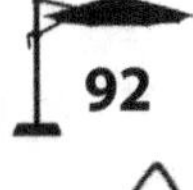

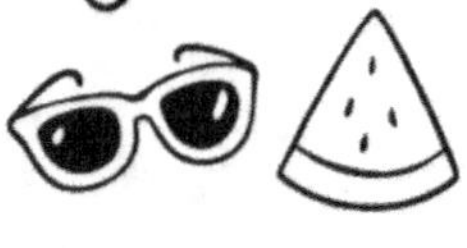

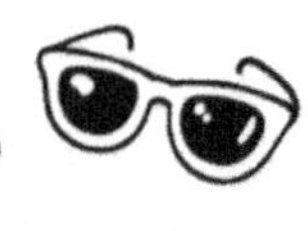

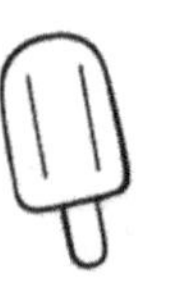

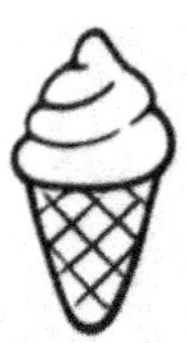

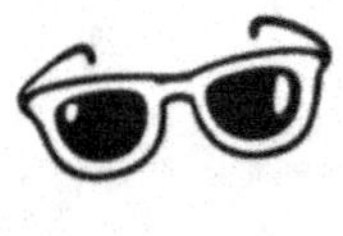

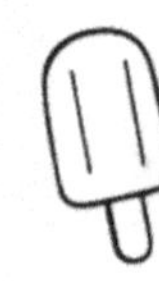

My Summary Wellness Check

Area	*How Am I Doing?* *(Circle One)*	One Thing I Could Improve
Sleep	Terrible / Okay / Great	
Moving my body	Terrible / Okay / Great	
Eating okay	Terrible / Okay / Great	
Screen time balance	Terrible / Okay / Great	
My mood most days	Terrible / Okay / Great	
Time outside	Terrible / Okay / Great	

My One Health Goal

- *If you could improve ONE thing about how you take care of yourself this summer, what would it be and why?*

____

____

____

____

____

Who I Go to When I'm Struggling

- *Sometimes we need help - not just a snack or more sleep, but real support. Who are the people you can go to when you're having a rough time?*

____

____

____

____

GETTING READY FOR WHAT'S NEXT

The end of summer is actually a really important time. How you finish summer affects how you start the new school year. The best way to head into fall is with your head up - not scrambling at the last minute.

What Is Coming Next for Me?

- Describe what the transition back to school or to fall looks like for you:

____

____

____

____

____

What excites me about it	What worries me about it

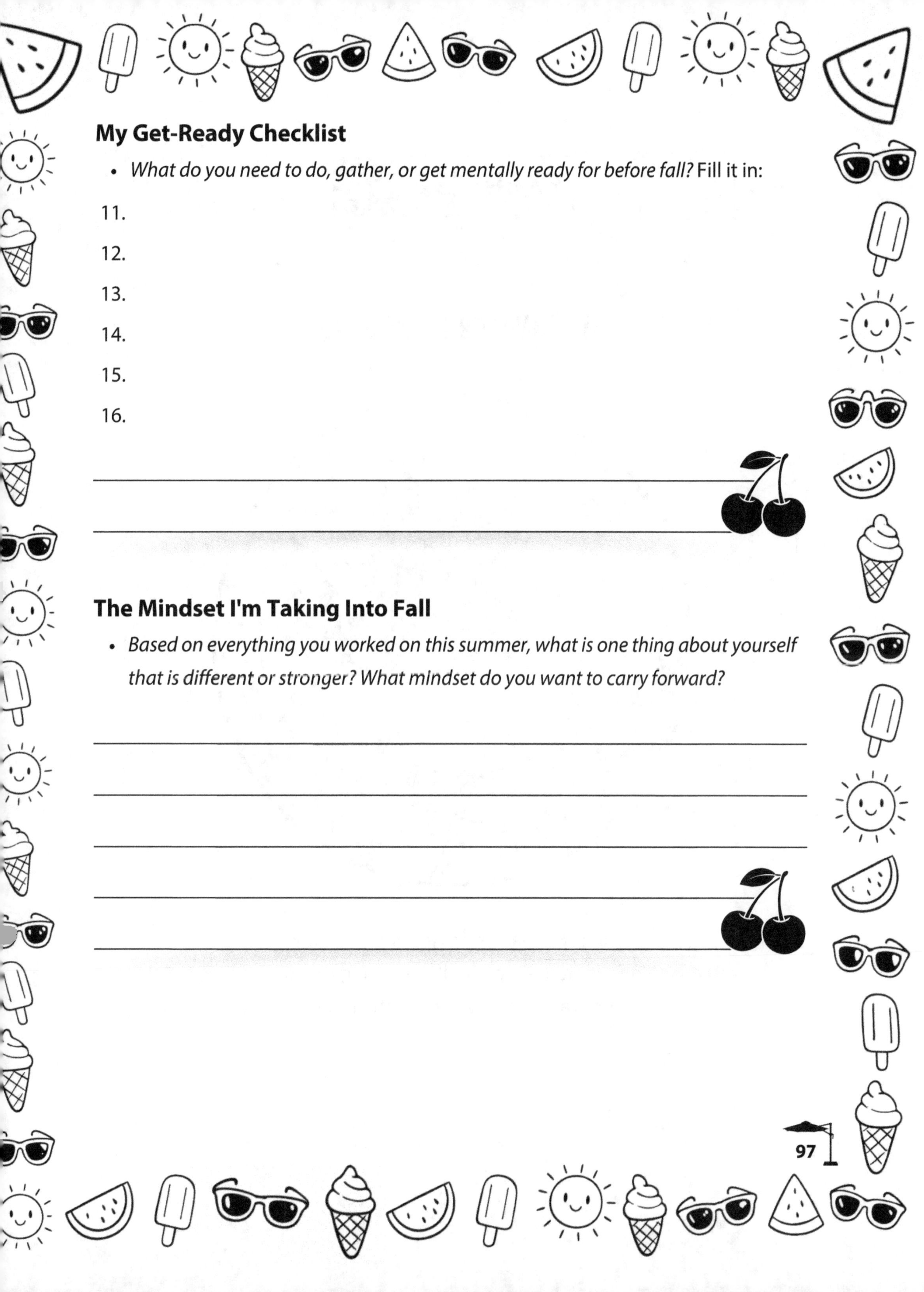

My Get-Ready Checklist

- *What do you need to do, gather, or get mentally ready for before fall? Fill it in:*

11.

12.

13.

14.

15.

16.

The Mindset I'm Taking Into Fall

- *Based on everything you worked on this summer, what is one thing about yourself that is different or stronger? What mindset do you want to carry forward?*

MY SUMMER GAME PLAN

This is your last exercise - and your most
important one. Let's pull everything together
into a real plan you can actually use.

My Top 5 Takeaways From This Workbook

- *What are the 5 most useful, surprising, or interesting things you discovered about yourself?*

1. _______________________________________

____

2. _______________________________________

____

3. _______________________________________

____

4. _______________________________________

____

5. _______________________________________

____

My Summer Commitments Table

Area	What I Will Do	By When
Know Myself		
Take Charge		
Look Around		
My People		
Smart Choices		

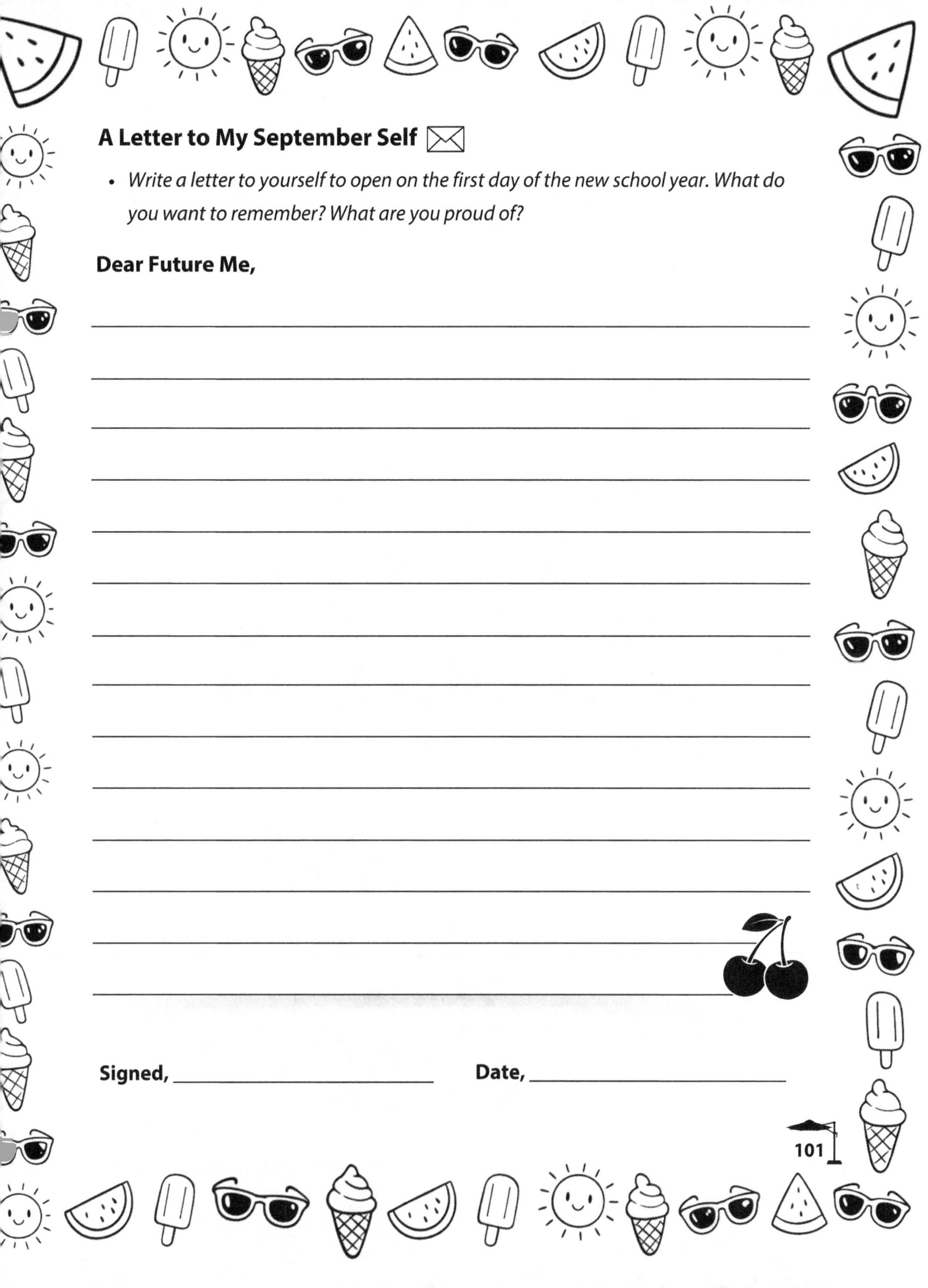

A Letter to My September Self ✉

- *Write a letter to yourself to open on the first day of the new school year. What do you want to remember? What are you proud of?*

Dear Future Me,

____

____

____

____

____

____

____

____

____

____

Signed, _______________________   **Date,** _______________________

CONCLUSION

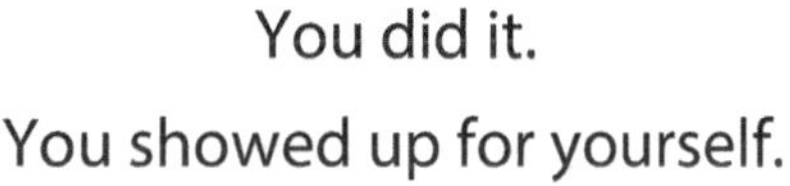

You did it.
You showed up for yourself.

Whether you worked through every single page or just dipped in here and there, you put in real effort to understand yourself better. That matters more than you know.

Here is something to remember: the skills you practiced in this workbook - knowing yourself, managing your time, caring about others, building strong friendships, and making smart choices - are not just summer skills. They are LIFE skills. You will need them in September, next year, and every year after that.

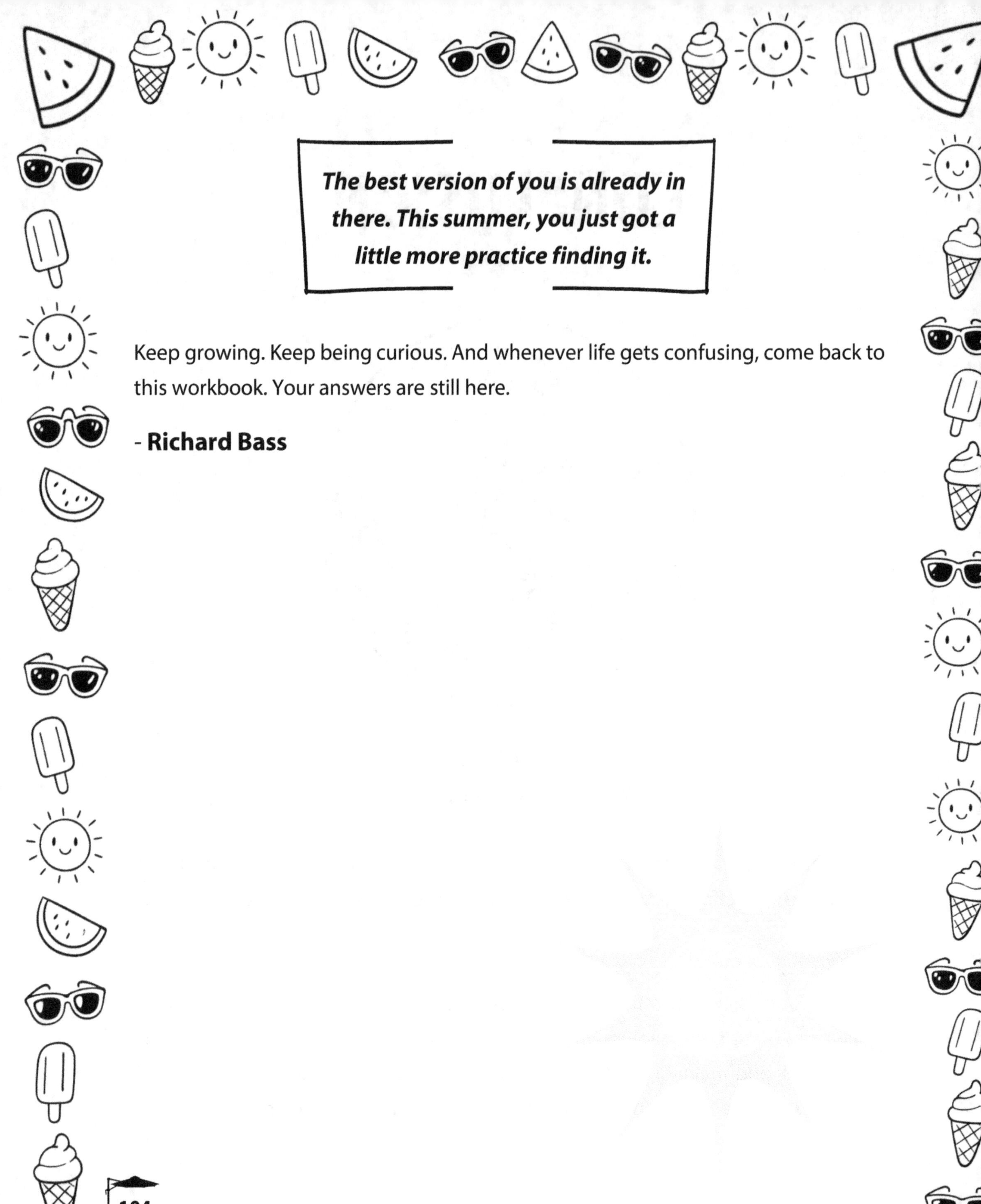

> **The best version of you is already in there. This summer, you just got a little more practice finding it.**

Keep growing. Keep being curious. And whenever life gets confusing, come back to this workbook. Your answers are still here.

- Richard Bass

ABOUT THE AUTHOR

Richard Bass

Richard Bass is a special education teacher, bestselling author, and advocate for neurodivergent youth and families. With over 20 published books and more than 100,000 copies in print through RBG Publishing, Richard has built a reputation for creating practical, accessible resources that meet young people where they are.

His work spans social-emotional learning, ADHD, autism, sensory processing, oppositional behaviors, and teen mental health. He writes for educators, parents, and teens themselves - always with the same commitment to honesty, respect, and usefulness.

- **Website:** *richardbassauthor.com*
- **Instagram and TikTok:** *@richardbassauthor*
- **YouTube:** *Thriving with Richard Bass*

A MESSAGE FROM RICHARD BASS

To every teen who picked up this workbook:

I wrote this for you specifically - not for your teacher, not for your parent. For you.

This workbook was built differently. It assumes you are capable of deep self-reflection. It assumes you can handle honesty. It assumes you already have the answers to a lot of these questions - you just need the space and the right prompts to find them.

Summer is a particular kind of invitation. It asks you: *what do you do when no one is making you do anything? Who are you when the structure falls away?*

That question is worth answering. And the fact that you are trying to answer it - through these pages - says something real about you.

Keep growing. Keep being honest with yourself. I'm rooting for you.

- Richard Bass

REFERENCES

- **CASEL (2020).** *CASEL's SEL Framework. casel.org*
- **Bandura, A. (1977).** *Self-efficacy: Toward a unifying theory of behavioral change. Psychological Review, 84(2), 191-215.*
- **Dahl, R.E. (2004).** *Adolescent brain development: A period of vulnerabilities and opportunities. Annals of the NYAS, 1021(1), 1-22.*
- **Duckworth, A. (2016).** *Grit: The Power of Passion and Perseverance. Scribner.*
- **Dweck, C.S. (2006).** *Mindset: The New Psychology of Success. Random House.*
- **Goleman, D. (1995).** *Emotional Intelligence. Bantam Books.*
- **National Scientific Council on the Developing Child (2015).** *Supportive Relationships and Active Skill-Building Strengthen the Foundations of Resilience. Harvard University.*
- **Seligman, M.E.P. (2011).** *Flourish. Free Press.*
- **Siegel, D.J. and Payne Bryson, T. (2011).** *The Whole-Brain Child. Delacorte Press.*

BONUS

QUICK TIPS CHEAT SHEET

5 Things to Remember All Summer Long

Skill	The Summer Challenge	Quick Reminder
Know Yourself	Less structure to define your day	Check in: how am I actually feeling today?
Take Charge	Too much free time can become wasted time	One goal + one routine = a great summer
Look Around	It is easy to get stuck in your own bubble	Someone near you might need a kind word
Your People	Friendships drift without effort	Send the first text. Show up. Be consistent.
Smart Choices	More freedom means more decisions	When in doubt, ask: will I be proud of this?

When Things Get Hard This Summer

If You Are Feeling...	Try This:
Bored and stuck	Exercise 2.5 *(What to Do When I'm Bored)*
Stressed or anxious	Exercise 2.4 *(Dealing with Summer Stress)*
Left out by friends	Exercise 4.1 *(Keeping Friendships Going)*
Pressured to do something	Exercise 5.2 *(Saying No to Peer Pressure)*
Unsure about a decision	Exercise 5.1 *(Should I Do It?)*
Fighting with Family	Exercise 4.3 *(More Family Time)*
Unsure about a decision	Exercise 5.6 *(Getting Ready for What's Next)*

Remember: *You have everything you need inside you. This workbook just helped you find it. Have an amazing summer.*

3 FREE Bonuses!

- **Positive Discipline Playbook:** Dive into 50 powerful strategies designed to unleash your child's full potential through positive guidance. Say goodbye to tantrums and hello to harmony!

- **Kids' Planner:** Get organized and empower your child with this fun and interactive planner. From homework schedules to goal-setting, watch them blossom with confidence!

- **The Positive Self-Talk Guide:** Help your teen transform negative thoughts into powerful affirmations! This practical toolkit includes daily exercises, reframing techniques, and 50+ positive self-talk starters. Watch them shift from self-doubt to self-confidence!